THE ARCHIVES FRANCO STOLE FROM CATALONIA

The campaign for their return

COMISSIÓ DE LA DIGNITAT
THE DIGNITY COMMISSION

The Archives Franco Stole from Catalonia
The campaign for their return

Prologue by Josep Bargalló
Preface by Artur Mas

editorial
MILENIO
LLEIDA, 2004

© Comissió de la Dignitat, 2004
© For this edition: Editorial Milenio, 2004
   Sant Salvador, 8 - 25005 Lleida (Catalonia, Spain)
   editorial.milenio@cambrescat.es
   edmilenio.com
First edition: October 2004
Legal inscription: L-886-2004
ISBN: 84-9743-129-4
Printed at Arts Gràfiques Bobalà, S. L.
Printed in Catalonia, Spain

INDEX

PROLOGUE

Although in this day and age we have other means of conserving historical memory, until not long ago we used to say — in Catalan — that «words are blown away by the wind» and that only papers are true guardians of the past. Documents have been, over the centuries, the physical expression of the way in which nations lived, thought and felt. They are their most direct historical will. They are the agents that have bequeathed to posterity the events that our forefathers experienced. That is why documents have become an essential means of understanding and evaluating historical memory. Without papers, without documents, we would be orphans with regard to our past. Thanks to them, we can identify ourselves as a clearly defined nation.

It can therefore be of no surprise to anyone that the Catalan people should want to recover the documents that bear witness to the country's age-old identity. No nation may steal from another elements which are essential to making up its history; no nation may steal from another the cultural trappings that sustain its memory. It is for this reason that the people of Catalonia call today for the return of what was taken from them as a symbol of submission, as war spoil taken on their defeat. If there is a true will to build a State of brother nations, in which the respect for the plural nature of the different historical communities involved is to be truly guaranteed, the historical memory of these nations must also be maintained. To turn a blind eye to their demands is to spoil the chance of furthering dialogue and the possibility of peaceful coexistence. It also shows a will to continue maintaining the symbols of defeat. The documents retained at Salamanca stand for much more than mere historical heritage. They show the on-going state of submission which the Catalan people were exposed to in 1939.

In all awareness of this fact, the Parliament of Catalonia, on May 18th 1989, passed Resolution 73/III, on the recovery of documents held at Salamanca. As a result of this petition, on March 15th 1995, the Spanish Government's Cabinet decreed the return «without further delay» of the Civil War documents to their rightful owner, the Catalan Generalitat Government. However this step was not taken because of the opposition that was met with in certain areas of the administration, a reactionary attitude which received the backing of the more centralist and conservative media. A new Resolution of the Catalan Parliament (155/VI), on June 1 2000, has still not met with a favourable solution.

Over the last three years — 2002-2004 — the submission to opposition and the failure to meet the demands of our institutions have been seen by the Dignity Commission — Comissió de la Dignitat — as a blatant lack of respect for our country. This has been the motive behind the task this organisation has carried out creating awareness and calling for support, an initiative that has met with vigourous response throughout the world and in the most select cultural fields. This book is the showcase of work carried out by the Dignity Commission in defence of our dignity as a nation. We must be grateful for the efforts made in the hope that this question will shortly be rewarded with the only possible solution it demands: the return of all the Catalan and Valencian document funds to their rightful owners, one of whom is the Catalan Generalitat Government itself.

Josep Bargalló i Valls
Catalan Prime Minister

PREFACE

While this book is of immediate interest to the people of Catalonia, I am convinced it will also interest all those who firmly believe that co-existence between nations is based on the principle of justice. This book addresses unresolved problems that we have inherited from the saddest period in the history of 20th century Spain. It informs us about the pillaging of Catalan family, business and institutional archives by the forces of occupation that were led by the rebel general who subsequently became the dictator Franco. The book explains how the confiscated documents were removed to Salamanca and used in a wave of repression against those committed to the advance of democracy in the Spanish Republic, particularly those who had done so to defend their linguistic, cultural and political identity as Catalans. It also throws light on our long-standing and unsuccessful attempts to reclaim these archives. Moreover, it will show us that we are not alone in condemning this unjust situation: we have gained the support of distinguished people across Spain, Europe and throughout the World. This fact encourages us in our efforts to further press the Spanish government to repair an injustice committed by an invading army and an unlawful government.

The Dignity Commission is the driving force behind this initiative. It has united people of good will and a number of initiatives under its banner and has achieved great success in familiarizing the people of Catalonia with the issue of the «Salamanca Papers». This has been accomplished using a strong civic approach, two aspects of which I would like to highlight for their special importance. The first is the educational approach adopted by the Commission as it has set out to explain the issue to people and to convince them — whether those at home, impressed as they have been by the Commission's efficient, persistent and well — organized work, or others further afield who have been impressed by the need to return the stolen materials and by the advantages to be gained in doing so. It has largely meant an attempt to reverse the consequences for those who were conquered but not convinced. In seeking to restore things to their rightful place, the Commission wishes to convince rather than conquer. The second aspect I would emphasize is the Commission's success in involving so many important figures around the world in an exemplary expression of solidarity and support of a just cause wherever in the world one is to be found.

Artur Mas
Former Catalan Prime Minister

INTRODUCTION

The phenomenon born in the wake of the Dignity Commission's[1] struggle for the return to their rightful owners of the so-called «Salamanca Papers» — stolen by Franco's men 65 years ago — is remarkable for various reasons.

The first and foremost is that of having managed to achieve a very wide degree of unity of action between people, organisations, trade unions and political parties from the most varied of backgrounds, ideologies and geographical origins, joining them together in an initiative that was immediately to receive the full support of Catalonia's major institutions of government.

A second factor would be that the Dignity Commission, while exposing the wide distance that sadly still exists today between the perception of democracy held by Catalans and Spaniards, has at the same time contributed to the establishment of productive links with groups in Castile and Leon, groups which have seen the Catalans not as the «traditional enemy» — as is the custom — but as a very real ally in the vital task of recovering historical memory and pushing aside the demagogy that has until now hampered understanding and solidarity between nations.

To this we must add the fact that — as several observers have pointed out — the Dignity Commission, on gaining wide support for the first International Manifesto in summer 2002, has helped to place the «Salamanca Papers» scandal on the agenda throughout the world.

---

1. In Catalan, Comissió de la Dignitat.

In this introduction it should also be explained why the book has two prologues, one by the present Prime Minister of the Catalan Generalitat government, Mr Josep Bargalló, and one by his immediate predecessor, Mr Artur Mas. The reason for this is that Mr Mas was Prime Minister at the time when this book first received the government's support, an attitude that has been fully confirmed by the current government. Our gratitude to both. We must also point out that this book is reaching you after considerable delay due to the intensive electoral agenda Catalonia has faced since 2003. Our apologies.

In this introduction, we would also like to thank all those people who, from abroad, have taken an interest in this question and sent their support for the Dignity Commission's Manifesto of June 2002 which sought to uncover one of the last remaining stains that fascist Europe has bequeathed to the XXI Century. In gratitude, we are sending you a copy of this book as originally promised. We wish to thank many of you for the messages of support largely received by e-mail.

We would also like to express our gratitude for the right to use photographs taken by Rafel Tixé — official Dignity Commission photographer — Ignasi Aragay (head of the culture section at newspaper *Avui*), Pere Virgili (*Avui*), Fermí Esteve (Palau de la Generalitat), Félix Corchado (*La Vanguardia*), Agustí Ensesa (*La Vanguardia*), M. Lorenzo, Mané Espinosa (*La Vanguardia*), Marc Garrofé (*La Mañana*), Toni Alcàntara (*La Mañana*), Ivan G. Costa (*El Triangle*), Tim Abrahams, Colin Mearns and Cristina Calderé (*Avui*). Our thanks too to newspapers *Avui* and *La Mañana*, as well as to the Catalan Government's Presidency Departament and the Universitat Catalana d'Estiu (Prada) for generously allowing us to reproduce images they ceded to us. We would also like to thank cartoonists Lluís Puyal and Fer (*Avui*) for letting us reproduce their hilarious cartoons which are included as a small sample of the hundreds of «Salamanca cartoons» that have appeared in the Catalan press in recent times, themselves a subject worthy of a book. Our deepest gratitude too to Henry Ettinghausen, Stephen Telfer and Joe Linehan for translation work, valuable proof-reading and suggestions that were most welcome. Parallel to this, we also want to show our gratitude to publishers Editorial Pagès and to the Catalan Government for their keen support.

This book was designed and written by a score of people who are in some way associated with the Dignity Commission's Secretariat: Imma Albó, Anna Almazan, Josep Altayó, Agustí Barrera, Enric Borràs, Xavier

Borràs, Josep Camps, Emília Capell, Josep Cruanyes, Henry Ettinghausen, Joaquim Ferrer, Julià Garcia, Josep Guia, Montserrat Milian, Rosa Maria Puig-Serra, Paula Ros, Marta Rojals, Agnès Toda, Toni Strubell and Ramon Vilardell. All of them wish to dedicate this book[3] to the real heroes of this story, namely the hundreds of thousands of men and women who suffered death, emprisonment, exile and massive confiscations at the hands of the Francoists for the only reason that they had defended Catalonia, freedom and democracy against fascism.

Barcelona-Valencia, October 2004

---

2. For further information, consult the Dignity Commission web: http://www.partal.com/dignitat.

CHAPTER I

HOW THE DOCUMENTS WERE STOLEN

On 26 April 1938, Ramón Serrano Suñer — Franco's minister of the interior and great admirer of the Nazis — signed a decree creating the National Department for the Recovery of Documents (DERD). This body was responsible for the confiscation of documents from Republican organisations, parties, trade unions and many other types of association that had been deemed to be «contrary to the National Movement» and that were seen as «likely to provide the State with information on the activities of its enemies». These documents were to be confiscated from the premises of these institutions and bodies as soon as Francoist troops occupied territory that had originally remained loyal to the Republic.

This decree did little more than formally institutionalise a body which had been created the year before and which had begun its activities during Franco's campaign against the Basque Country and the northern territories. It was on this campaign that several task groups carried out search operations as soon as new territory was occupied. Confiscated materials were transported to DERD'S centre which had been set up in Salamanca, the most important and safest city[1] in the power of those who had rebelled against the Republic. The confiscated documents were processed and sieved for information that would provide the Francoists with details about the political and social activities of thousands of citizens, and so allow them to carry out a merciless campaign of repression. These details were then passed on to the police and other political departments as well as to the military courts.

From the beginning of its activities in the Basque campaign, DERD was composed of search teams that were to set up document collection points. The first such centre was in Bilbao, where a search team was to

---

1. Due to its proximity to dictator Salazar's Portugal, an ally of Franco.

15

extract data and pass it on to the bodies responsible for repression. Its main task was to seize documents from the Basque Country's institutions of self-government. They confiscated one hundred and thirteen boxes that were found in the port of Santander where they were awaiting shipment to France. From its Bilbao office, the information section also gathered information on the location of organisations in towns that had not yet been occupied to facilitate the task of the search teams on arrival. At the Salamanca headquarters, the central classification and record office staff were responsible for processing data and establishing a records office which subsequently led to the creation of five hundred thousand data cards by the end of 1938.

Although documents were confiscated both from Basque and Republican institutions, it is noteworthy that those belonging to people and businesses supporting the rebels were returned to them. Among the institutions targeted by DERD, the following are significant:

1. Military affairs.
2. Domestic policy (law and order, evacuees, social work).
3. Foreign intervention (refugees, material aid, personal and moral support, propaganda, foreign correspondence).
4. Culture and propaganda (public education in general, sports, lectures and public events, propaganda and activist involvement).
5. Justice (civilian courts, imprisonment, sentences, forced labour).
6. Political parties (PC, PS, PR, JSU, FAI; accounts and minutes).
7. Separatism (Basque, Catalan, Galician and Valencian political parties and institutions associated with the nationalities, universities, etc.).
8. Economy (department of confiscations, treasury, provisions).
9. Trade Unions (UGT, CNT, AIT, SOV).
10. Covert activities (DERDI, Friends of the USSR, support committees, anti-fascist leagues, organisations associated with women's liberation, naturism, esperanto, literary/scientific clubs, etc.; sports, sects; theosophism, freemasonry).

After the campaign in northern Spain, Catalonia was to be the main target of the Francoist forces since it had a Government and Parliament of its own. Furthermore Barcelona, the capital of Catalonia, was at that time the provisional seat of the Spanish Republican and Basque governments. The operations of the search teams working on the

Aragonese front began to be perfected. In Catalonia, they were first to be active around the Lleida, Terra Alta and Montsià regions as far as the boundary marked by the Segre and Ebre rivers, where the front line persisted for months. All the seized documents were held either at the Lleida or Vinaròs centres.

From its base in Salamanca, the information service prepared a list of search operations to be carried out in Barcelona. On 24 December 1938, over one thousand nine-hundred locations had been listed and assigned to one of ten different police districts which were to cover over six hundred streets according to the plan the occupation forces had drawn up for the city. They had also decreed that on entering Barcelona, DERD staff would occupy premises at Via Laietana 54, a building placed at this organisation's disposal by the Insurance Company La Equitativa.

After the Battle of the Ebre, at the end of December 1938, the final offensive on Catalonia was launched, and frontline search teams began operating in areas occupied as of 8 January. Starting on the Lleida plain, they moved towards Tarragona by way of the counties of Conca de Barberà and Camp de Tarragona. Searches led to a haul of 135 sacks, a further 33 sacks in Igualada and others at Vilafranca del Penedès and Sant Sadurní d'Anoia.

Franco's men occupied Barcelona on 26 January 1939. The next day, police and military forces took charge of the city, which was placed under martial law until May. Franco's forces were accompanied by frontline search teams. A small DERD detachment had been left at Salamanca to guard its premises there, but the remaining staff of fifty, including its director Marcelino Ulibarri, the heads of the investigation teams, the office staff, archivists and auxiliaries, were all moved to Barcelona. In addition, fifty soldiers from the Second Corps of Navarre's Carlist troops were brought in as auxiliary staff, increasing to one hundred the men involved in search operations in Barcelona and the rest of Catalonia. About ten commandeered vehicles were used to transport search teams and confiscated documents.

Two days after the occupation of Barcelona, on 28 January, the six search teams began to work at full capacity, bringing in sacks of documents by the lorry-load. They were stored at fourteen premises that had been occupied for the purpose. DERD headquarters was to be at Muntaner 265, and its garage at Llúria 153. Among the premises used for storage, the Catalan Parliament building was to be a prominent one. It was also used as a base for the military police accompanying the occupation forces, whose General, Eliseo Álvarez Arenas, set up his headquarters in the Palau Robert, a building that formerly housed the Catalan Ministry of Culture, and which was situated at the junction of avenues Diagonal and Passeig de Gràcia. The army of occupation's court set up its offices in the Justice Palace, formerly the seat of the Catalan Supreme Court of Appeal.

About two thousand search operations were carried out throughout the city, the last taking place on 7 June 1939. Although only about three hundred searches were made in February, these operations were to yield the largest booty. Most of the searches were carried out in March, however. From that month on, the number of staff in Barcelona was reduced because some of its members were sent off on new offensives that would lead to the fall of the remaining Republican fronts in Madrid and Valencia. In the first few days, activities were focused on the more important newspapers, magazines, bookshops and printing presses. It was also a priority for them to seal off premises used by the Catalan government as well as those used by the Republican and Basque governments. Their premises were searched and documents removed over the following days. As they scoured official buildings and the headquarters of the major parties and unions, search teams also began to inspect the homes of those party and union leaders suspected of concealing important documents. After searching the Generalitat Palace — the seat of the Catalan Government — they also started to sift through the homes of councillors, members of the Parliament of Catalonia as well as the President of the Catalan Parliament himself.

From the Barcelona office they continued to organise the spoliation operations in the rest of the State as well as activities which involved the drawing up of political record cards that were then made available to the police and the military courts engaged in a full-scale campaign of repression. Because the volume of documents seized was so immense — lorry-loads of sacks were brought to the stores daily — it was impossible to process it all as it came in, despite the large team dedicated exclusively to the task. That is why they decided to take the most significant documents, lists or information cards from each place they searched, as this material was more likely to supply them with the data they sought. It was all subsequently processed by the office and sent daily to the different agencies of repression.

As in Bilbao, the DERD set about returning documents and private libraries to owners whose materials had been confiscated during the war period. They were normally conservatives who had gone over to the Francoist side. That is why Barcelona newspapers published lists of people who could retrieve their documents after swearing allegiance to Franco and after receiving the approval of local Falangist leaders. The bodies responsible for political persecution — both the police and the Falangist militia — confiscated documents during search operations. All documents were subsequently passed on to the DERD, which organised inspection operations on a centralised basis.

The destruction of books and journals

One of the duties of the occupation forces was to confiscate all books and journals considered to be contrary to the spirit of Franco's National Movement. This was not only the responsibility of DERD but also that of the Falangists' Department of Press and Publicity, a body responsible for their elimination or «purge» — to use the Francoist term — from all public libraries, cultural institutions, publishers' offices and bookshops. DERD withdrew ten copies of each book or journal it found; the rest were pulped. As historian Josep Cruanyes has been able to confirm, the profits from the sale of this material to paper mills were set aside to fund DERD's activities. In Barcelona, this body is known to have destroyed at least seventy-two tons of published material. The total amount destroyed in the first months of the occupation of Catalonia was much greater because the massive volume of books destroyed by Falange's Press and Propaganda Department must also be taken into account.

In the first few days of operations, the offices of the following newspapers were searched: *La Batalla, El Treball, Solidaridad Obrera, La Publicitat, La Veu de Catalunya, El Diluvio, El Día Gráfico, La Noche, La Humanitat,* as were those of magazines such as *Tiempos Nuevos, Moments, La Revista Blanca, Mujeres Libres.* The same occurred at the bookshops Catalònia, Bosch, Bastinos and Castells, as well as at the majority of publishers and printing presses. As regards political parties, large-scale searches were made at the offices of Esquerra Republicana de Catalunya, Partit Socialista Unificat de Catalunya, Acció Catalana Republicana, Estat Català and Unió Democràtica de Catalunya. The offices of the anarchist groups Confederació Nacional de Treball (CNT) and Federació Anarquista Ibèrica (FAI) were also searched. Of the other trade unions, large-scale searches were also made of the premises of Unió General de Treballadors (UGT) and the Centre Autonomista de Dependents del Comerç i de la Indústria (CADCI). At some trade union headquarters, such as those of CNT, FAI or CADCI, search operations lasted a full week, and several lorry-loads of sacks containing documents were removed.

Search operations were conducted at the following cultural institutions: Ateneu Barcelonès, Ateneu Enciclopèdic Sempre Avant, Ateneu Enciclopèdic Popular, the Ateneu Politècnicum, Gran Teatre del Liceu, Institut de Cultura i Biblioteca Popular de la Dona; choirs such as L'Orfeó and L'Eco de Catalunya; sports clubs, or associations such as Associació Protectora de l'Ensenyança Catalana, where the Apel·les Mestres children's library was closed down and the Catalan-language *History of Catalonia* for Catalan school children was destroyed. We also know of searches conducted at minority religion centres — such as those of theosophical or spiritualist congregations — as well as at naturist clubs such as Pentalfa, run by Italian-born professor Nicolas Capo, who also published a magazine and several periodicals on healthy nutrition. DERD removed his complete library and over a ton of back numbers, all of which were pulped.

Among the locations where most documents were confiscated, one must include the different offices of the Catalan government. From the Catalan Economy Council alone, at Rambla Catalunya 83, four lorry-loads of documents were taken on 22 and 23 March 1939. Among the more severely affected parties were Esquerra Republicana de Catalunya, whose different offices were targeted in sixty search operations, and Partit Socialista Unificat de Catalunya, targeted in ninety search operations. At one of the offices of PSUC, situated in Gaudí's Pedrera building in Passeig de Gràcia, twenty-two sacks of documents were taken. As regards the unions, both the Confederació Nacional del Treball and its sister anarchist organisation, Federació Anarquista Ibèrica, were subjected to very thorough search operations. One hundred and fifty CNT offices in Barcelona were searched. At CNT headquarters on Via Laietana 32, the search lasted for a week. The search of the FAI's headquarters at Via Laietana 30 also took a week. Eight lorry-loads of documents were removed from these offices. Another union that was subjected to a major search operation was the Centre Autonomista de Dependents del Comerç i de la Indústria, a nationalist union with a solid tradition and a long heritage that included different services and co-operatives belonging to its members. The search at the central offices at Rambla Santa Mònica 25 also lasted a week and led to the confiscation of one hundred and eighty sacks of documents. This gives us an idea of the size of the confiscation operations that took place, a phenomenon without precedent in Catalan history.

The Freemasons

Parallel to DERD, another body was founded called Servicios Especiales, which was designed to confiscate all documents found on premises run by the Freemasons. Servicios Especiales was also headed by Marcelino Ulibarri. In Barcelona, this section's Guardia Civil agents searched the Fènix Atheneum Club in the Portal de l'Àngel, which was the headquarters of the Gran Logia del Noreste and the Lògia de Catalunya amongst others. Of the forty-one search operations carried out at the homes of Freemasons, those taking place at Roc Boronar i Font's — a member of the Logia Liberación who later joined the Logia Themis — are significant. In these operations, care was taken to confiscate all kinds of symbolic objects associated with Masonic rites, ranging from the clothes of members to the furniture on the premises. Today it is still possible to visit a mock Masonic lodge installed in the Archive in Salamanca. It contains a display of objects associated with the Masonic rite, exhibited in a way designed to mock the organisation's practices. It is incomprehensible that the installation was not dismantled once democracy returned and its contents handed back to their rightful owners. How can a democratic society maintain a propagandistic exhibition aimed at attacking a particular ideology? It is disturbing that this is allowed by the very State that ought to guarantee respect for freedom of thought. However, visitors are given no explanation as to why this display is still in place.

The last period of the Barcelona office and the move to Salamanca

In March 1939, arrangements were made to move the head office to another building in the city, at Carrer Princesa 21, where there was plenty of space available for the archive, with a large basement for storage. When it became apparent that no more search operations were to be carried out, and after various fronts had fallen, which lead to the accumulation of thousands of tons of documents, Ulibarri ordered all the documents to be sent to Salamanca on 24 May 1939. Meanwhile a liaison office was to remain open at the new head office. Packing operations were begun and DERD's different offices in Barcelona were closed down, including the main office in Carrer Muntaner. There were estimated to be about 3,500 sacks of documents in eight warehouses across the city, along with those stored at the head office. The material taken from the Freemasons had already been sent to Salamanca by lorry.

Over the course of several days, as many as twelve railway wagons were loaded with documents and trains loaded with documents are known to have left for Salamanca between 21 June and 5 July 1939. In all, over one hundred and forty tons of documents were to be transported. The Tarragona, Igualada and Lleida documents were sent direct to Salamanca in military vehicles. The Barcelona office remained open until September, when an order was given to move the central office to Salamanca. The transfer of office documents and files was carried out on 8 October. The last occasion on which documents were brought to Barcelona from other Catalan cities was 13 February 1940. We can thus conclude that, in all, over two hundred tons of documents were confiscated in Catalonia.

Operations elsewhere in Catalonia

As explained above, the document confiscation teams conducted search operations in some Catalan towns between April 1938 and January 1939, when the Francoists were advancing eastwards towards Barcelona. In February 1939, once efforts were centred on the Catalan capital, Marcelino Ulibarri posted a memorandum to all Catalan municipal corporations ordering them to send all their documents associated with the Republican period to DERD offices. Due to the varying degrees of efficiency and compliance within the different town halls involved, the results were to be quite inconsistent. However, at least one hundred and fifty Catalan town halls are known to have sent documents to the DERD office in Barcelona.

Operations in the Balearic Islands[2]

DERD did not confiscate any material in the Balearic Islands. The main reason for this may be that the order to confiscate materials was not

---

2. For operations in Valencia, see the section on «The Office in Valencia» in Chapter 3.

issued until mid 1937 when Franco's army had already taken over in places such as Majorca. In the first few days after the fall of the largest Balearic island, most of the documents the Francoists laid their hands on were destroyed. Another factor was that DERD teams did not actually arrive on the islands of Eivissa and Menorca until later.

At the service of repression

Most of the documents had already been transferred to Salamanca in the first few months of 1940 when Marcelino Ulibarri boasted that he had 800 tons of documents stored in Salamanca's Dominican monastery. It was here that all the sacks had been taken from the various fronts. These figures illustrate the magnitude of the fascist regime's confiscation operation that even surpasses that carried out by the Nazis in Germany.

After the war ended and when all the documents confiscated in the last Republicans zones had been seized, the task of reorganising them was undertaken. There was not to be a classification process as such, but documents that might contain references to suspects' ideological leanings were to be selected. For those searching for information, it would suffice to find references to individuals in publications or discover that they were members of a co-operative or a republican club. On finding this data, investigators would compile an information card with the name of the person and the document kept in a folder as «proof» of the «crime» committed. Sometimes the cards were created for seemingly ridiculous reasons such as the fact that the suspect had given money to an association raising funds to aid the victims of the bombing raids on Lleida in western Catalonia (1938). To find a suspect's name in a communist newspaper justified the creation of a card. The classification process was carried out to create a police record office and no professional archivistic criteria were respected, leading to the chaotic distribution that still exists today.

About one hundred people were involved in this task, many of whom lived in San Ambrosio, the school building which was later to become the police headquarters in Salamanca. The processing operation is known to have lasted until 1958. An enormous collection of documents — including three million personal cards — was to be the result. This police records office compiled political reports that were sent on to military courts, special «political responsibility» courts — which exerted financial repression — and the courts for the purging of civil servants.

Such courts sought to rid the administration of those of its employees who had not shown «leanings» towards the new regime.

Apart from what was to be termed the archive of «political and social records», the Servicios Especiales section established a records office containing 190,000 cards, hundreds of personal records and thousands of reports on the Masonic links of suspects. Among the documents considered to have Masonic connotations, it is surprising to find those of groups wholly unrelated to the Freemasons, such as the Jewish community of Barcelona, the Evangelist Church, the Rotary Club or other spiritualist or theosophical organisations. This confusion can only be understood in the light of the fact that the Francoists received the support of influential sectors of the Catholic Church that were fiercely opposed to the Freemasons, seen as key actors in the «plot» of what was termed the «Jewish-Freemason alliance» against the «Traditional, United and Catholic Spain» that the Church defended.

The Salamanca records office was also to supply material to a new political court called the Special Court for the Repression of Freemasonry and Communism (TERMC), which had the ever-present Marcelino Ulibarri as its first president. It judged people for having held posts in Masonic groups or political parties. The court brought charges on the basis of reports compiled by the DERD. TERMC was later substituted by the Public Order Court (TOP), which was created by a law of 2 December 1963. TERMC continued to exist as a court for political repression until the end of the Franco regime in 1975, however.

At the death of Marcelino Ulibarri, the DERD changed its name to Delegación Nacional de Servicios Documentales (DNSD), a term it would retain until its dissolution by way of a decree issued on 28 October 1977. Thus ended a body that had been a vital piece of Franco's repressive regime. It had no *«raison d'être»* after the legalization of the unions, political parties and the restitution of the Catalan Government, bodies which it had sought to repress using information gleaned from the archives it had confiscated.

The documents now held in Salamanca

The institution we know today as the «General Civil War Achive» of Salamanca is in fact the archive of the National Office of Documentary Services (DNSD), a body that had had its head office in the old San Ambrosio school in Salamanca before being dismantled. It was the archive created by the administration when the confiscations started. It had a Masonic section called Servicios Especiales and continued its activities until the body replacing it — Servicio Documentales — was dismantled. Amongst the documents it holds are the correspondence and documents generated by the centre. These include a huge collection of three million police cards and 190,000 information cards on the Freemasons. There are also thousands of reports drawn up during the centre's active period. When called for, these documents were farmed out to different State departments as well as to the TERMC itself. They often failed to be returned. When all is said and done, what today is presented to us as the «Archive of the Civil War» is indeed little more than what one historian described as a «glorified police records office».

To get an idea of what is still conserved there, twenty-nine years after the death of Franco, it is worth studying the evolution of the centre over the last sixty-six years. In 1940, when an attempt was made to move DERD from Salamanca to El Escorial, a site nearer Madrid, DERD documents were calculated to weigh about one thousand tons, a factor that militated against the transfer. Little is left today of those documents, largely made up of the eight hundred tons of unclassified sacks stored in Santo Domingo in Salamanca. This can be verified by studying the inventory of the classified batches. It reveals that, apart from documents, the following items had also been confiscated: books, magazines, periodicals and many other objects such as official stamps, posters, paintings, sculptures and other miscellaneous objects. In the case of Masonic centres, a special effort was made to confiscate all sorts of symbolic elements such as furniture, clothes and other ritual objects associated with the network and its members.

From studies carried out on the documents still held in the collection at Salamanca, it appears that when they were sorted, many were either destroyed or sent on to form part of other collections in the Francoist state. One of these destinations was the Military History Service, where documents of a military nature were sent. Many books confiscated by DERD and held in the Archive were later to be sent to the libraries of Francoist institutions such as the Political and Social Section of the police. Another destination for the documents was the «Causa General», an inventory of «crimes» attributed to the Republicans and drawn up by the Franco regime. As it was much less convincing than Francoist propaganda had made out, it was never published.

It is now known that there are Catalan Government Justice Department documents in the National Archive in Madrid[3] which had been extracted from the DNSD office in Salamanca. There is a suspicion that important confiscated documents now missing from Salamanca may also have been transferred to other State bodies.

All this leads us to conclude that not all the confiscated materials have been conserved and that many materials have been forwarded to other institutions. The fact that countless documents have been destroyed is proven by studies showing that when the confiscated documents were processed, several tons of paper classified as «useless» were extracted and used to produce data cards and paper needed in large quantities to draw up records and reports in the records office.

If we consider the volume of documents taken from Catalonia, we must sadly conclude that only ten percent remains of the originals. The rest was either sent to other State archives or destroyed in large quantities. Twelve railway wagons full of documents left Barcelona in 1939. Today, what remains would barely fill one, however. Another fact proving that documents were destroyed is the knowledge that several lorry-loads were also confiscated from the Catalan Government's Economic Council in Rambla Catalunya. Today there are only nineteen batches mentioned in the inventory of documents held in the Civil War Archive in Salamanca. This shows that many documents were not conserved in Salamanca, as one is led to believe, but actually destroyed.

One factor we may find surprising about the distribution of documents in batches is the apparent lack of order that exists among the documents used to create the data cards. It seems that they should have been classified according to the bodies or private individuals from whom they were confiscated, but the truth is that the order in which they were kept depended on the repressive aim towards which the organization worked. The people responsible for selecting documents and sifting through books and other publications later filed them in the order in which they had been handled. On the cards, they wrote a reference to the place where the documents had been stored, hence the apparent disorder. In fact, the order that exists in the Archive is that of a police records office.

---

3. Indeed, they form part of its index of documents.

The archive is organised under a series of headings. In the case of the Catalan documents, the headings are «Lleida», «Barcelona» and «Vinaròs», the original confiscation points during the Catalan campaign. However, the shortcomings of the filing system are reflected in the fact that Catalan documents are also found among the batches in Madrid. This shows that the idea that documents were to be filed on the basis of the place where they had originally been confiscated was not respected. This was probably due to the carelessness of the staff, largely underqualified police agents. Another possible reason for the deficient filing system is the chaos there must have been in the large sack-filled store at Santo Domingo.

When the confiscations took place, many of the victims had already fled and those who had not were either in prison or were to act as mere on-lookers as DERD agents conducted their search operations. These agents failed to identify themselves or give any reason for the confiscations. Indeed, the DERD was a secret police corps that, while it kept internal reports, did not receipt those affected when it conducted its operations. The State gave out no official information about the Salamanca records office. Those who had suffered confiscations were offered no information, a factor which helps to explain why so few victims knew the whereabouts of their documents. This has been put forward as a reason for the fact that many victims have not been able to claim their belongings until now. As the contents of the records office are increasingly made known, a growing number of descendents of those who suffered confiscations are discovering that their documents — or part of them — are still kept in Salamanca. The State must be seen as fully responsible for the fact that such people have been unaware of this until now. The Spanish government should have returned all remaining confiscated materials to the victims years ago. The failure to do so explains why it has been almost impossible to reconstruct the archives of so many institutions or individuals, as has been the case, for example, with the legitimate Catalan Government or the heirs of the former Vice President of the Catalan Parliament, historian Antoni Rovira i Virgili. In the case of political institutions such as the Government or Parliament of Catalonia — both suppressed for thirty-nine years — no record was kept of the destinations of the documents confiscated from them. Even today, no pre-1939 Catalan Parliament document is held by Catalan institutions except for a very small number that were fortunately saved by Parliamentary officials.

Classifying the Catalan Government documents required examination of thousands of batches of documents kept in sections corresponding to different sources. It also meant painstakingly cataloguing documents and replacing them in their original order. Even then it is evident that many documents are missing. Some may have been dispersed to other collections such as the «Causa General» (the General Cause that was an attempt to list all «red crimes»). Many other documents were destroyed during «classification» operations at the Salamanca police records office.

In the case of documents confiscated from proscribed parties, trade unions or other social and cultural organisations, all records that could have led to the identification of their origin were eliminated. Currently, none of the major Catalan trade unions — CNT, UGT, CADCI — are in possession of their pre-1939 archives. The same is true of the major parties whose histories have been written on the basis of press reports but without the aid of their official records that are scattered amongst different document batches in Salamanca.

As regards the kind of documents involved, among those belonging to individuals we find materials ranging from private correspondence, correspondence between intellectuals or politicians to complete libraries such as those confiscated from Antoni Rovira i Virgili, Antoni Xirau, Joaquim Maurín or Nicolas Capo. Surprisingly enough, in a police or political records office such as this, we also find a full set of Catalan literature dating from the end of the nineteenth century to 1939. The only explanation for this is that they are books written in Catalan, a factor that was considered «dangerous» by the State and a language persecuted the State.

In the last few years of its existence, the Documentary Services body of the Francoist administration denied any involvement in the confiscation of the belongings of the former Vice President of the Catalan Parliament, Antoni Rovira i Virgili. This became apparent when his daughter, Teresa Rovira, requested the authorities to return them to her in the last few years of the Franco regime. In contrast, the private documents of several Spanish Republican politicians, such as Giner de los Ríos or Azaña, have been duly returned to their respective families by former Spanish governments. Among the remaining documents, most have absolutely nothing to do with the Civil War because all documentation referring to the war was selected and transferred to the Military History Archive. The remaining documents, apart from those associated with public affairs and institutions, are of very varied origins. There are documents ranging from private letters and books belonging to various private libraries, to different kinds of documents belonging to political, social and cultural organisations and trade unions. Many of these documents do not even belong to the Republican period. Numerous Atheneum (literary or scientific) clubs or trade unions had their archives dating back to their foundation in the nineteenth century confiscated! One example of private documents stored in Salamanca is that of those confiscated from the surgery of the Barcelona-based Italian doctor Nicolas Capo, a specialist in alternative medicine. Kept there is the correspondence he maintained with patients and the health questionnaires filled in by those he visited prior to the prescription of suitable diets. All the documents date back to the twenties, a period prior to the proclamation of the Republic, let alone the Civil War! It must also be pointed out that if more descendants of the victims of confiscation have not come forward to demand their documents, it must be due to the fact that they simply did not know that it was a body called DERD which had looted their archive or library. Logically, it was the State's responsibility to inform those affected about remaining documents. The State's tendency to conceal the archive's contents and the fact that it has granted archive status to a police records office must be seen as spurious ploys aimed at gaining precious time. It is a dishonest strategy designed to avoid returning documents that the Francoist State had been able to retain only by brute force.

Today it is a paradox that the State has still not returned the confiscated documents to those who demand them. It highlights the fact that the Francoist regime treated its supporters better than the current democratic State treats its citizens today. Until the confiscated material is returned, the Spanish State will not have fulfilled its duty of ensuring justice for those citizens who were persecuted by the Francoist regime, a factor that leads many Catalans to question the democratic credentials of the Spanish State. This issue also brings to mind the fact that one of the debts associated with the wounds caused by the civil war and the Franco dictatorship has yet to be paid: a public tribute to all those who suffered persecution by Franco and who are still ill-treated today. As stated by the authors in the introduction, this book is dedicated to them.

CHAPTER II

THE CLAIM, 1978-2002

The Catalan claim

When General Franco died in his bed in the autumn of 1975, it looked as if the cruel dictatorship that he had imposed for nearly forty years might well just cave in. What actually followed was the period known as the «Democratic Transition», which involved the re-establishment of democracy and therefore the possibility of self-government for Catalonia. It was a period during which the people irrepressibly asserted their rights in all spheres of life. Amidst the uncertainties and the obstacles facing the struggle for freedom, one of the claims that were made from the outset was the need to preserve the archival heritage and, in particular, to recover the archives that the Franco regime had seized from the Catalans in 1938 and 1939.

The first steps

On 18 January 1978 the well-known historian and politician Josep Benet[1] put a question in the Spanish Senate on the need to preserve the archival heritage in its entirety in view of the measures being adopted at that time by the Minister of the Interior, Rodolfo Martín Villa.[2] These measures involved the destruction of archives belonging to political organisations that had fought against the Francoist dictatorship. Benet stressed the crucial importance of such documents for writing the history of the period and demanded that they be put in order with the help of archivists and historians. His call also sought to prevent Francoist

---

1. The senator to have received most votes at an election in modern Spanish history.
2. Former leader of the Falangist students' union at the University.

organisations from burning their own archives in response to an order issued by Villa. The minister replied to Benet that no steps had been taken to do away with documents of any nature.

Josep Benet's question alerted public opinion to the need to ensure the continuity of the archival heritage at a time when the struggle to regain democracy was a priority. Unfortunately, it did not prevent the Minister of the Interior from having a large portion of the archives of anti-Francoist political organisations destroyed. It has been possible to prove that this operation took place when historians who wanted to study the Franco period found that the documents they were looking for had been destroyed.

However, the general feeling during those first uncertain years of the Transition was a will to have the archives that had been seized by Franco returned to their rightful owners. The first parliamentary step in this direction was taken in the Spanish Congress on 25 March 1980 by Antoni de Senillosa, an MP for Coalición Democrática.[3] He presented a motion which called the Ministry of Culture to reclassify the «Salamanca Papers» «on the basis of logical criteria for their consultation by experts», and «with a view to their transfer to the Catalan Government». It was prefectly clear at that time that even Spanish right-wing parties believed the «Salamanca Papers» would be returned to the Catalan people. However, the calling of new parliamentary elections made it impossible to debate and pass the motion and thus, most probably, to solve a problem that, from that moment on, turned into a never-ending story.

Catalan unanimity and the first Spanish refusal

On 17 July 1980, at the initiative of Max Cahner, the Minister of Culture of the Catalan Government, historians Manuel Mundó and Jaume Sobrequés were to visit the building in Salamanca that houses the stolen archives. In the report that they drew up, they asserted: «We have been able to visit this Archive, get a general idea of its contents and see what came from the Catalan Government, its Ministries and Departments, as well as from Catalan civic, political and cultural institutions and from towns and cities in Catalonia.» They stated that each section of the vast

---

3. Curiously enough, this group's spokesman was Manuel Fraga Iribarne, former Francoist Minister of the Interior and currently President of Galicia.

depot included large quantities of documents associated with all fields of Catalan political, social and cultural life. As for the staff running the depot, they wrote: «The only person who works there is the Secretary, Pedro Ruiz Ulibarri, who was wounded in 1938 during the Civil War. Although he is not a qualified archivist, he knows the Archive very well because he has been working there for the past forty years. His only assistants are a secretary and two porters. Security is seen to by two Civil Guard agents.»

A few months later, on 17 December 1980, the Catalan Parliament debated the question of the «Salamanca Papers» for the first time. Josep Benet, who was then a member of the Catalan Parliament, asked about the Catalan Government's efforts to have the papers returned. In addition Benet proposed that an inventory be made of the Catalan Government documents held in the archives of the Spanish State[4] with a view to their return. In his reply, Max Cahner defined the priorities of the Catalan Government in this field.

On 11 April 1983, Xavier Folch, an MP for the PSUC, raised a question regarding the documents. He criticised the agreement that had been signed with the Spanish Ministry of Culture on 22 October 1982 for the microfilmimg of the archives of the Catalan Government. He argued that, instead of announcing that it had achieved the return of the Catalan Government archives held in Salamanca, the Government had announced that it had signed an agreement «which, in our opinion, totally contradicts these statements, because in that agreement [...] the Spanish Ministry of Culture behaves as if it were the owner of those archives, merely allowing the Catalan Ministry of Culture to microfilm archives which are the inalienable property of the Catalan Government.»

In his reply Max Cahner spoke of the Madrid Government's refusal to return the papers:

> My Ministry's objective obviously centred on obtaining the original documents, whose ownership, we believed, lay with the Catalan Government, as well as those other documents that were confiscated from Catalan institutions, bodies and individuals during the final years of the Civil War and in the immediate post-war period. The Spanish Ministry of Culture — the various Ministers of successive administrations in that

---

4. Especially those stored in the Salamanca records office.

Ministry — absolutely refuses to contemplate the return of the originals [...]. What we did manage to obtain from the Ministry is the concession — it isn't often that one can achieve such a thing, but we did — to allow us to have a microfilm copy (financed, what is more, by the Spanish Ministry), and we considered that we ought to accept that as a first step because, at least whilst our claim for the return of the originals proceeded, our researchers in Catalonia would be able to have access to the documents on microfilm.

The question was next raised by Josep Lluís Carod-Rovira, MP for Esquerra Republicana de Catalunya (ERC), and was debated in the Cultural Policy Commission on 18 May 1989. He made his intention abundantly clear:

The point of our motion is this: to recover for the people of Catalonia archival material that belongs to them, by virtue of both its institutional and its private heirs — material that is essential for the understanding and the analysis of the history of our country and that needs to be made available to all those who wish to consult, study and publish it.

The text of the motion, which was passed unanimously, read as follows:

Resolution.

The Parliament of Catalonia calls upon the Spanish Government to continue [...] the procedures relating to the recovery of the archival material seized in Catalonia as a result of the Civil War so that it can be consulted, studied and disseminated at the National Archive of Catalonia and other organs of the Catalan civil service in the following ways:

First. By undertaking and completing, in every case, an inventory of the entire body of material that originated in Catalonia and was held in Salamanca in the Civil War Section of the Spanish National History Archive.

Second. By continuing to demand of the relevant State authorities the return, and deposit in the National Archive of Catalonia, of the archival material that refers to the Catalan Government under the Spanish Republic that has already been inventoried.

Third. By consulting all the civil service organisations of Catalonia, as well as the rightful owners of the materials held in Salamanca, regarding the future location of those materials.

Fourth. By investigating, through the Catalan Ministry of Culture, precisely which archival materials held by the Spanish State should be returned to Catalonia.

On 16 May a motion had been put to the Spanish Parliament by the Catalan Minority group. It was signed by its spokesman, Miquel Roca i Junyent. Its text read: «Parliament calls upon the Spanish Government to undertake the procedures required in order to return to the Catalan Government the archival materials, held and classified in the Salamanca section of the National History Archive, that were seized during the Civil War.» The motion was debated on 28 June by the Education Commission of the Spanish Congress. When the representatives of the other parliamentary groups spoke, those of CDS and Partido Popular (PP) supported the return of the documents, whilst the Partido Socialista Obrero Español (PSOE) spokesman — Mr. Paniagua — came out against this view, asserting:

> Gentlemen, I believe that, since in Salamanca we have managed to house one of the best archives in the world relating to the Civil War, and have even recovered documents from abroad, it would be a mistake to destroy its unity in order to satisfy the perhaps legitimate wish to hand them over to the Catalan Government [...]. Our group feels unable to support this motion, and we fail to understand how other groups can support it [...]. Taking into account the interest of the public at large and of researchers in particular, the unity of the History Archive of Salamanca, belonging to the National History Archive, must be maintained. Consequently, this group will vote against the motion.

As at that time the PSOE's absolute majority was overwhelming, the vote went against the return of the «Salamanca Papers».

Return rejected again

On 25 February 1992, Joaquim Ferrer, a member of Convergència i Unió (CiU) in the Spanish Senate, put the following question to the Minister of Culture, Jordi Solé Tura: «Does the Minister, the person responsible for the National History Archive of Salamanca, intend to return to the Catalan Government the documents that the Franco dictatorship's political repression seized from it?» Minister Solé Tura replied:

> I have to say that, personally, I am entirely in agreement with what you suggest [...]. It seems perfectly reasonable, justified and right that, now that legitimacy has been re-established, things should be returned to precisely those places from which they should never have been removed. On this, therefore, I am fully in agreement. The only problem — and I cannot pretend that it is not a serious one — is a technical one.

One year later, on 30 March 1993, noting that the matter had proceeded no further, Senator Joaquim Ferrer laid another question before the Minister of Culture: «Is it true that the Minister finally intends to return to the Catalan Government the documents that were seized from it by the political repression of the Franco dictatorship?» On this occasion Solé Tura reaffirmed «*the unity of the archive*» and suggested that the solution to the problem lay in the new technologies. It was clear that there was enough political good will to resolve the question.

On 11 November the Esquerra Republicana de Catalunya (ERC) members of the Catalan Parliament tabled a motion «concerning the recovery of the archival materials seized in Catalonia as a result of the Civil War.» Presenting the motion before the Cultural Policy Commission, Mr. Carod-Rovira stated: «It would be a matter of collective shame if what the Franco regime united by force could not now, under democracy, be separated by exercising freedom.»

The two debates held in the Spanish Congress a few months later were very different, and they ended in the Socialist government refusing to effect the return of the «Salamanca Papers». The first of these debates took place in the Education and Culture Commission, on a motion tabled by IU-IC. The motion, signed by Rafael Ribó, read as follows: «The Spanish Congress calls upon the Government to carry out the return to the Catalan Government of the documentation held in the History Archive of Salamanca so that it may be housed in the National Archive of Catalonia».

Pere Baltà, on behalf of the Catalan group, recalled the example of the return, on 22 December 1989, of the photographic archives of the Catalan Government's Propaganda Committee following a motion presented in the Senate by CiU. He ended his speech by pointing out one of the basic problems that had prevented the return of the «Salamanca Papers»: «Our impression is that the reason why these documents have not been returned to Catalonia is not a political one, but a politico-technical one: that is to say, a problem originating in the highest reaches of the Spanish State archives, as a result of which a cultural heritage that, according to the criteria of UNESCO and any number of other bodies, ought to redress a historic injustice is not in fact being given back to Catalonia.»

Gómez-Alba Ruiz, in the name of the conservative Popular Party (PP), spoke against the motion, as did the socialists, who still had a majority in Parliament, with Jesús Caldera arguing against the motion in the same terms as the PP. When the vote was taken, the socialists and the PP combined to reject the motion.

A few months later, on 14 June 1994, the Spanish Congress debated a new motion presented, this time, on behalf of the Mixed Group, by Pilar Rahola. Aware that the question had been aired only a few months earlier, she said:

> One day the lawfully constituted State will return the archives of the Catalan Government to the people of Catalonia, their rightful owners. The sooner that happens, the sooner we shall be able to close a wound that is still open in Catalonia and that will remain so until we recover this part of our heritage.

When the time came for other groups to speak, Pere Baltà asked, on behalf of CiU: «What is this archival unity we keep hearing about? What exactly is it that is supposed to be fragmented if these documents are handed back? This is a matter of fundamental justice and basic rights. In fact, it is a question of the moral righting of a looting operation carried out with military violence by the overweening pride of a victor whom history has defeated.»

For the socialists, Jesús Caldera spoke in terms that recalled those he had used only a few months earlier, ending with the following assertions: «Wherever the Spanish National History Archive is located, only the Spanish State can be responsible for its custody. In conclusion, it is clearly an archive that belongs to the State and must therefore be run by the State.»

In the space of just a few months, the Catalan claim for the return of the «Salamanca Papers» had been flatly rejected twice.

Very close to return

In the 1994 elections to both Houses, the socialists lost their absolute majority, and this enabled Convergència i Unió to obtain a series of concessions in exchange for giving qualified support to the PSOE government. Amongst the concessions obtained was the return of the archives of the Catalan Government of the 1930s. On 17 March 1995, the Spanish Cabinet was informed of the imminent agreement to hand the archives back, and the press announced this as a fact. The following day, the Catalonia section in *El País* carried the headline: «Government Returns to Catalan Government the Catalan Government Archives of the

Republic,» and the article explained that, «after fifteen long years of argument, the Cabinet decided yesterday that the original papers of the archives of the Catalan Government under the Republic that were seized by Franco's troops as the spoils of war be handed back to Catalonia [...]. The Catalan National Archive at Sant Cugat will house the originals now held in Salamanca.» Unfortunately, however, weakened by a series of other problems, as well as scandals, the socialist government proved incapable of resisting the opposition to the transfer that was unleashed.

The Mayor of Salamanca, the socialist Jesús Málaga, announced that he would «defend the unity of the archive, tooth and nail,» whilst the President of the PP in Salamanca, Julián Lanzarote, made it clear at a press conference that he was prepared to «physically prevent a single document of any historical importance leaving the archive» (*La Vanguardia*, 21/03/1995). On 21 March, in view of the opposition to the transfer, Carmen Alborch beat a retreat, determining that the Spanish Parliament be charged with taking a decision that could perfectly well have been taken simply by ministerial order. That very day the Mayor of Salamanca, Jesús Málaga, «ordered the chief of police to keep a watch on the archive, day and night. In his orders, issued after a plenary meeting of the City Council, he told his men to let him know immediately if they detected any documents leaving the building» (*ABC*, 23/03/1995). After a meeting with the Mayor, the Minister declared that «at the last meeting of the Cabinet the Government had approved the request made by the Catalan Government on numerous occasions. It is a matter of returning the papers to their rightful owners, and I can see no reason to oppose this» (*El País*, 24/03/1995). For his part, the Mayor called for «a silent demonstration through the streets of Salamanca, ending up at the National History Archive» (*La Vanguardia*, 25/03/1995).

On 30 March, the demonstration called in Salamanca to protest against the return of the papers took place. It was reported as follows in *Avui*:

> The demonstration, which began on time at 8.30 p.m. and rapidly covered the established route, was led by the bearers of a large banner that had been hung from the City Hall bearing the slogan: «The City of Salamanca in Defence of the National History Archive.» Some 15,000 to 25,000 people took part in the demonstration, the largest ever held in the city, according to City Council sources, who actually spoke of as many as 55,000 demonstrators. Be that as it may, the main square was filled to overflowing. The demonstration was headed by the chief political and cultural authorities of the city, led by Mayor Málaga (*Avui*, 31/03/1995).

After a speech read by the mayor, the 84-year-old writer Gonzalo Torrente Ballester spoke, inviting the people of Salamanca to «show love for what is yours by right of conquest.» Understandably, these words were met with considerable irritation in Catalonia, and the following day, when Catalunya Ràdio briefly interviewed Torrente Ballester, he stated: «I wasn't referring to the archives of the Catalan Government. I was talking about archives relating specifically to Salamanca: the Cathedral archives, the University archives, the College archives, which are genuinely Salamanca archives. The rest are here, but don't come from here.» «Why, then, did the people of Salamanca come out onto the streets,» he was asked by Antoni Bassas of Catalunya Ràdio. «I don't know. I didn't go out with them. They came to my house to fetch me […]. They asked me to say a few words in support of the Salamanca Archive staying here, that's all,» he replied. «So would you be prepared to allow the return of the Catalan Government archives?» he was asked. «Look, there's nothing like that here. From what I've been told, there's nothing here that has anything to do with the Catalan Government under the Republic. As far as I know, the only thing here is material about the International Brigades.»

On 4 April, Prime Minister Felipe González reaffirmed, on Iñaki Gabilondo's «Hoy por hoy» programme on the Cadena Ser radio station, that he was «absolutely behind the restitution of the Catalan archives confiscated at the end of the Civil War,» though he also insisted that it could not be implemented «until analyses and studies have been completed to determine whether there is any objection from a technical or scientific viewpoint.» It was obvious that he was beginning to look for an excuse not to return the «Salamanca Papers».

Further refusals

On 25 April 1995, PP Senator Julián Lanzarote, now Mayor of Salamanca, put a question to the Minister of Culture, demanding to know «whether the Archive would remain in Salamanca,» to which she replied: «I can assure you that we are going to seek […] a consensus, because I believe that the question has never been dealt with, either in Parliament or elsewhere, with the complexity that it demands.»

That very day she had received from the mayor of Salamanca the signatures of 97,000 people who opposed the return of the papers to Catalonia.

On 10 May, Senator Lanzarote attacked again by presenting a motion to the Senate that produced an angry debate. Lanzarote himself actually defended the unity of the Salamanca Archive on the basis of orders decreed by Franco during the Civil War. The motion was defeated, but it was clear that the question of the return of the papers had reached a new impasse. Carmen Alborch went on making apparently positive statements, but it was obvious that the intention was simply to gain time. Thus, on 4 May, at Santa Coloma de Gramenet, she declared that the Civil War Section of the National Archive would remain in Salamanca, «independently of the possibility that, by agreement, some documents might be transferred to Catalonia» (*El Periódico*, 05/05/1995).

The question of the return of the papers was entering a stage identical to those that had been reached so many times before. The State-wide political parties spoke in accordance with what they perceived to be their immediate interests, often actually contradicting themselves and incapable of defending energetically or consistently the just claims for the return of the papers.

Another attempt: the Commission of Experts

On 28 May 1996, the Spanish Congress passed a motion put forward by the Mixed Group, and in particular by Pilar Rahola, of ERC. After a long debate, during which several amendments were made, the following motion was approved: «This House calls on the Government to hasten the work of the commission of experts that was set up in the previous session so that, within the next six months, it can produce a report on the papers generated by the Catalan Government during the Second Republic which are held in the History Archive in Salamanca and propose solutions for their location, whilst at the same time guaranteeing the archive's integrity by the appropriate technical means.» It might have looked as if the possibility of their return was being opened up, but two days later Margarita Vázquez de Parga, who had been confirmed in her post as head of the State Archives by the new PP government, made a statement that did not bode well: «I believe the commission may be of some help. I don't believe this is the right moment to say anything decisive, but, like all the archivists I know, I am totally against the dismembering of the Archive» (*El País*, 30/05/1996).

The commission of experts was set up on 10 July by the Archive Board as a «specific sub-commission», presided over by the new Minister of Culture, Esperanza Aguirre. Its members were: Santos Julià, Antonio Elorza, Javier Tusell and Josep Fontana, and they had access to «the expert advice of other specialists, such as Margarita Vázquez de Parga and Fernando Rodríguez Lafuente, the Director General of Books» (*La Vanguardia*, 11/07/1996). On 11 September, Javier Tusell accused the Minister of «messing the commission about,» in view of the fact that her Ministry was taking the business «at a snail's pace» and had not allowed the commission access to papers that were «essential in order to address the question» (*El País*, 01/09/1996). The Secretary of State for Culture, Miguel Ángel Certes, announced that he would «make a formal investigation in order to determine whether negligence could have brought about 'the delay in the provision of the texts — technical information on inventories — that had been asked for by the Commission on Archives in order for them to be able to pronounce on the transfer to Catalonia of the documents claimed by the Catalan Government'» (*Avui*, 16/09/1996). A few days later, Margarita Vázquez de Parga declared that she was «vacating the post of chief authority on archives in the Ministry of Culture that she had held for the past ten years» (*Avui*, 18/09/1996). She had, in fact, been the real obstacle, blocking all the initiatives that had been attempted during that entire period.

On 27 November, the commission of experts completed its report, points 5 and 6 of which stated:

> Five. This Commission, within the limits defined as to its scientific competence, in accordance with the instructions of the Spanish Congress, and insofar as legal advice and the constitution allow (art. 149, 1.28; art. 132.3 of the Constitution, and art. 28.2 of the Law on Historical Heritage), puts forward the possibility of effecting a deposit of documents currently in the Civil War Section of the National History Archive at such archival institution as may be decided in agreement with the Catalan Government, in its capacity as an organ of the State.

> Six. The precise contents of this deposit would have to be decided by the Trust [of the National History Archive] on the advice of the Technical Commission made up of members designated by the Trust and the Catalan Government.

Reactions were not slow in coming. Juan José Lucas, the President of the autonomous region of Castile and León, stated that «his government will appeal if the documents are transferred» (*El País*, 28/11/1996), and the Mayor of Salamanca made it clear that any such transfer «would

involve dismembering an archive that had been legally constituted»
(*Avui*, 28/11/1996). The following day, the Socialists and IU in Salamanca
backed the position taken by the Mayor and the President (*Avui*, 29/11/
1996). This was a real «*dialogue of the deaf,*» as Enric Ucelay da Cal,
Professor of History at the Autonomous University of Barcelona, put it
(*Avui*, 30/11/1996).

Three years later, seeing that no attempt whatever had been made to
implement the commission's report, Josep Fontana made the following
analysis: «There was a dispute. Those of us on the Archive Commission
were asked to supply a solution, which we did. There has been no attempt
to implement it. Because of the balance of parties in Parliament, political
will is lacking. Six years ago the PP lacked an absolute majority and
needed CiU» (*La Vanguardia*, 09/11/1999).

However, a few months later, it was demonstrated that it was indeed
possible to return Catalan papers that had been looted after the Civil War.
Under Royal Order 616/2001, some sixty items produced by Laia Films,
a film company that had been set up in autumn 1936, were actually
returned to the Catalan Government. This was simply further proof of the
reactionary position that had been adopted regarding the «Salamanca
Papers». Then, on 12 February 2002, at the seat of the Catalan Government,
the Basque President, Juan José Ibarretxe, and President Pujol presided
over a ceremony held to mark the return of important Catalan Government
documents from the period 1933-1940 that had been preserved during the
Franco dictatorship, first in the archive of the Basque Nationalist Party
and then at the Sabino Arana Foundation. The return of this extremely
important collection was warmly welcomed by President Pujol, who
made it clear that it was the responsibility of the PSOE and the PP «to
disarm those who hide behind the right of conquest in order to contend
that the papers held in the Salamanca Archive of the Civil War should
remain there permanently» (*El País*, 13/02/2002). For the present, they
still prefer to hide behind their lack of democratic courage and to cling to
the spoils of war.

The joint State-Generalitat Commission (2002)

Throughout the year and a half of work by the Technical Commission
set up jointly by the Spanish Ministry of Culture and the Department of
Culture of the Catalan Generalitat Government to come to an agreement
on the Catalan documents held at the renowned Salamanca Archive, the

four members of that body — professors Antonio Morales, Carlos Dardé, Borja de Riquer and Joan B. Culla — had a pact of discretion that would enable them to reach a consensus. Final agreement proved to be impossible but, in any case, the Commission finished its work and each side was able to regain the freedom to express its views regarding the controversial documents.

In this sense, articles and newspaper reports in different media — or «publicity reports» as Joan Culla called them — such as the one written in *El País* by Miguel Ángel Jaramillo (director of the Archivo de Salamanca), were the only source whereby the public were informed of «developments». The novelty was, according to the article, that the Salamanca Archive «had taken a great step forward. It has modernized its installations to such an extent that the archives are available for online internet consultation». As historian Joaquim Ferrer was to ask: «Internet? Even if there were some truth to it, how does one account for the fact that between February 2001 and June 2002, no one — not even the director nor the Archives Directorate nor the Ministry of Culture — thought to bring this new development to the attention of the Technical Commission that was debating the character and chronology of the documents conserved at Salamanca?» Indeed, iIf these records were available online, how was it possible that the Ministry itself had supplied the Commission members, as their sole resources, with the Inventories «de la Sección Político-Social Barcelona» and «de la Sección Político-Social Lleida», items that had been written up by policemen and Guardia Civil in 1948! These were documents that were riddled with mistakes and dubious beyond description. There were two hypotheses: either the Internet story was a mere rumour, or else an attempt was being made to boycott the work of the Technical Commission by denying it access to efficient resources. Readers may choose whichever of the two interpretations seems more plausible to them.

As part of a general strategy to confuse and warp public opinion, on July 1 Mr Jaramillo stated in *El País* that the teams for «document recovery» — for which read *spoliation* — that led to the creation of today's Salamanca Archive had not indulged in confiscation operations. They had not taken complete archives, he argued, but only from «documents previously selected to supply information on people», an interpretation that is altogether false. The truth is that the teams looted everything they could lay their hands on, including posters, books and the

Catalan flag seen in November 1975 acting as a dust cover for a typewriter. As Joaquim Ferrer pointed out, «what form of previous selection would account for the presence, among confiscated materials, of papers belonging to the Republican Union of Valls dating back to 1890, the Republican Centre of Reus in 1886, the Republican Casino of Igualada in 1893, correspondence from the Companyia Transatlàntica or documents belonging to the Foment del Treball Nacional dating back to 1925? Did the Franco regime want to lay charges for «offences» committed 40 or 50 years before? Did it aim to lump together reds, separatists, sea-faring merchants and businessmen from the conservative Foment Nacional in its repressive objectives? Or could it be that Mr Miguel Ángel Jaramillo takes us for idiots?».

There is yet further confusion created on this subject in *El País*. In an article entitled «Un antiguo error convertido hoy en polémica»,[5] it is suggested that the origin of the dispute and the Catalan demands lies in a mistake made by the Ministry of Culture in December 1982 when it allowed Catalan archivists to catalogue and collate all the Generalitat documents that had formerly been dispersed in almost 2000 different batches of documents held in the Archive. Joaquim Ferrer is adamant on this point: «Mr. Jaramillo is lying on two counts here: firstly because he knows full well that the Catalan claim is not limited to the documents that belong to the Generalitat Government. It also relates to all the documents created in Catalonia; secondly because he is fully aware that demands for the return of the stolen documents began to be made in 1977-1978, when the Spanish Parliament was reinstated, through a motion presented in 1979 by MP Antoni de Senillosa. These demands, made by parties of all political hues, have been made in every parliamentary session since then. Furthermore, the idea that to bring the Generalitat documents together in one block was a mistake, a false and artificial step, shows up the defensive tactics adopted by the Archive: that of perpetuating the chaotic muddle of documents held there, with its inextricable confusion of geographical, institutional and chronological sources. Grotesquely, Jaramillo now wants us to believe that the «original» order should be respected when no such order existed. Instead, disparate documents were hastily amassed».

---

5. «An old mistake today turned into controversy», *El País,* 16/10/2002.

If at the start of the period of democratic transition and the dismantling of the National Office for Document Services, the Salamanca papers were rapidly forwarded to the Ministry of Culture to form part (in May 1979) of the Civil War Section of the National History Archive, the Catalan demand did not lag far behind Spanish Government moves. After several newspaper articles brought the subject to public attention, the Barcelona MP of the party Coalició Democràtica, Antoni de Senillosa, presented a motion in Congress in May 1979 in favour of the return. A year later, it was the head of this political group, Manuel Garrotxa, who supported a bill calling for the Spanish Government to urgently reclassify the San Ambrosio archive by «adhering to logical criteria for scientific consultation», and to return to the Catalan Government «those documents which had formed part in the past of the Generalitat Government's archives».[6]

Over the course of the following fifteen years, there were endless parliamentary initiatives, negotiations between governments and technical contacts to obtain the return of the Catalan documents. Since the Spanish Government alleged a lack of order and catalogue work in the controversial archives, in 1982 the Generalitat Government and the Ministry of Culture signed an agreement, at the expense of the former, that allowed professional archivists to extract and reclassify all those papers associated with the Generalitat Government between 1931 and 1939 from the jungle of documents stored at Salamanca. In all, 507 document batches were made. There is a well-drawn up inventory of them[7] and, as from 1993, a microfilm copy has been held at the National Archive of Catalonia. The remaining documents are lost within the chaos that prevails at Salamanca.

At its meeting of March 17 1995, the Spanish Cabinet, presided over by Felipe González, finally agreed to return to Catalonia the Generalitat documents held in Salamanca. In the political situation of the day, marked by elections, the agreement sparked furious sectarian reaction and, in Salamanca, was interpreted as an offence; it even prompted a the large demonstration on March 30. In any case, the storm of protest blocked the Government resolution that was never published in the State Official

---

6. Boletín Oficial de las Cortes Españolas. Congreso de los Diputados. I Legislatura núm. 340-1, 16 April 1980.

7. M. Teresa Díez de los Ríos et al., *Inventari de la documentació de la Generalitat de Catalunya al Archivo Histórico Nacional, Sección Guerra Civil*, Barcelona, Generalitat de Catalunya, 1992.

Bulletin (BOE). The transfer of the issue to the local and regional political agenda further strengthened municipal and commercial resistance to any form of return of the documents.

After the political change that came about in 1996, and under the pretext of technical reasons, the devolution hypothesis was soon replaced by the possibility of a deposit arrangement that would safeguard the ownership of the documents by the Salamanca Archive. Despite this, the most important move on the part of the State was Royal Decree 426/1999, of 12 March, which, after considering the «importance of the Civil War in the history of Spain, as well as that of the years leading up to and following it», was to transform the General Spanish Civil War Archive of Salamanca. Despite the solemn nature of this phrase, no military or diplomatic documents were to be transferred to the «new» archive at Salamanca, nor were other war-related documents which to this day are deposited in Madrid, Avila, Alcalá de Henares, Guadalajara or Segovia. On the other hand, what that Royal Decree does provide is an additional legal protection against any Catalan demands.

Nevertheless, while parliamentary initiatives on this question were still being taken in Madrid and Barcelona, the ministers of culture of the Spanish and Catalan governments agreed in June 2001 to set up a bilateral Technical Commission which — in the words of Pilar del Castillo — «should see if some documents, from the point of view of the Ministry and without affecting the principle of archive unity, could be allocated to a new location, in this case, in Catalonia». Constituted at the end of 2001, the Technical Commission worked until June 2002 with the agreement that a part of the disputed documents should be deposited in Catalonia, although an agreement as to the physical volume and the chronological extent of the deposit could not be reached. Two different (though not antagonistic) reports were to result from the process. Both of them were completely overlooked by the Archive's board which, on 22 July 2002, took the decision «not to embark on any initiative that may involve the removal of documents from the Archive», thus deeming the affair closed. Despite the general rejection of this position in Catalonia, the Minister of Culture and the Partido Popular ratified this agreement in Parliament the following September.[8]

---

8. See the Senate minutes for 11 and 24 September 2002.

CHAPTER III

THE DIGNITY COMMISSION IS CREATED

Neither things nor institutions are created out of nowehere. Experience tells us that there is always someone behind the scenes who decides to put machinery into movement, especially if it is a question of starting up an intiative as bold and ambitious as that of the Dignity Commission, which had the sole objective of achieving the repatriation of the Catalan archives held in Salamanca. Indeed, the initiative did not appear out of the blue and followed a path clearly marked out by the dogged determination of its founders and those who had preceded them in this cause.

At the end of October 2001, Toni Strubell and Julià Garcia were to meet in Torredembarra, just to the north of Tarragona, and give birth to the idea of creating an independent organisation that would campaign for the return of the «Salamanca Papers». What ed to this decision was the news that had appeared in *El País* newspaper regarding the plans for an exhibition to be held as part of the events of Salamanca European Culture City 2002. According to the article, Catalan documents stolen by Franco's troops and retained at Salamanca since the end of the Civil War, would go on show.

In the forthcoming weeks, further internet data was put out about the afore-mentioned exhibition. Soon to take an interest in the question were to be editor Enric Borràs, his journalist brother Xavier Borràs — soon to be press officer for the group — and historian Josep Cruanyes. Cruanyes was at this time writing a book on the subject of the «Salamanca Papers».[1] It was decided that the time had come to remind fellow Catalans of one of the many wounds left gaping since the Civil War. Since 1995 — the

---

1. Josep CRUANYES, *Els papers de Salamanca. L'espoli del patrimoni documental de Catalunya (1938-1939)*, Edicions 62, pushlished in June 2003.

last period in which Catalan society had expressed more concern over this question — the matter of the «Salamanca Papers» had not commanded too much public attention. Efforts were now made to establish contact with intellectuals, journalists, historians, archivists, writers and cultural activists with a view to seeking their viewpoint as regards the possibility of launching a public campaign in favour of the repatriation of the Catalan documents from Salamanca.

At the end of December 2001, the promoters decided on a venue in Barcelona to prepare a first meeting with people from central Catalonia. The objective was to decide on a future programme. In the course of this encounter, at a café in Barcelona's Passeig de Gràcia, a venue was established for the foundation of the Comissió de la Dignitat: the 21 January 2002. It was to be held at the prestigious cultural institution known as the Ateneu Barcelonès — Barcelona's Atheneum Club — in Carrer de la Canuda, a street just off the Rambles in Barcelona. A working agenda was drawn up for the meeting as was an initial list of people to be invited for the event.

The first meeting of the Dignity Commission was thus held on 21 January 2002. The meeting room granted by the Ateneu for the meeting was full to the brim. Among those attending were people who had come under their own auspices, such as the Director of the National Archive of Catalonia, Mr. Josep Maria Sans i Travé, and others in representation of important cultural or political bodies such as Òmnium Cultural and Alternativa Verda, or institutions such as the Barcelona City Council's Officer for Human Rights — Ms Roser Veciana — or Mr. Josep Camps from the Catalan Government's Presidency Department, later to be a member of the Secretariat. During the meeting, the promoters of the initiative explained the reason for the venue, laying special emphasis on former initiatives associated with the same affair. Information was also given regarding the exhibition on the Salamanca European Culture City 2002 programme. It was at this first meeting that a name for the group was to be suggested, based on the term «Dignity» as used in a phrase uttered by Literature Nobel Prize-winner, José Saramago. He had defined a «nation» as the community of people who have «not yet lost their capacity for indignation». Clearly, despite the historical offence the failure to return the Catalan documents stood for, Catalans now had a chance to show that they had not «lost their capacity for indignation» over a question as acute as the on-going retention of the «Salamanca Papers».

papers de Salamanca
tacats de sang!

papers de la dignitat, papers per al record, papers per la memòria, salamanca blood papers, papers per un futur, papers per no oblidar, papers per la llibertat, papers per la història, papers espoliats, papers que demanen justícia, papers tacats de sang!

Comissió de la Dignitat

Intelectuales de todo el mundo exigen el retorno de los "papeles de Salamanca"

■ En sólo cinco meses de vida, la Comissió de la Dignitat para el retorno de los "papeles de Salamanca" ha logrado el apoyo de más de quinientos intelectuales de todo el mundo

JOSEP MARIA SÒRIA

BARCELONA.– Más de quinientos catedráticos y profesores de 205 universidades de 47 países, así como numerosas personalidades del mundo de la política, la cultura, la historia y el arte, han firmado la declaración promovida por la Comissió de la Dignitat para la devolución "sin más dilaciones" de los fondos documentales de diversas instituciones catalanas que, desde 1939, se encuentran en el Archivo de la Guerra Civil, en Salamanca.

Entre los firmantes, se hallan Noam Chomsky (Massachusetts), James Petras (Binghampton), Howard Zinn (Boston); los ex presidentes Francesco Cossiga (Italia) y Mario Soares (Portugal); los premios Nobel Rigoberta Menchú y Adolfo Pérez Esquivel; los historiadores Sebastian Balfour, David Blackbourn, John Dickinson, Henry Ettinghausen,

Chomsky, Preston, Cossiga, Soares y Pérez Esquivel se hallan entre los firmantes

Thomas F. Glick, Stanley G. Payne, Paul Preston y Allan Yates, además de personajes como Danielle Mitterrand, Mikis Theodorakis, Peter Gabriel y Moustaki.

Los firmantes también solicitan al Gobierno español que "reconozca la titularidad de los fondos a nombre de sus legítimos propietarios (...) y si no se avienen a esta justa convención, que suspendan y retiren de la programación de los actos que se celebran en Salamanca, la exposición 'Propaganda en guerra'", prevista para el próximo otoño, dentro de los actos de la capitalidad europea de la cultura del presente año 2002.

La presentación del manifiesto corrió a cargo de su coordinador, el profesor Antoni Strubell, y se realizó en el paraninfo de la Universitat de Barcelona, en un acto presidido por el rector Tugores, al que acompañaba el director general

Chomsky, Preston, Soares y Peter Gabriel, con la Comissió de la Dignitat   ARCHIVO

Todos los parlamentos coincidieron en reclamar los llamados papeles de Salamanca. Ettinghausen citó cinco motivos –moral, político, legal, comparativo y práctico– y se refirió a que las Naciones Unidas "han afirmado repetidas veces el derecho de los propietarios de documentos expoliados en tiempos de guerra a reclamar su retorno". El profesor británico finalizó recordando que los documentos se hallan en el antiguo convento de San Ambrosio, santo que en el siglo IV se opuso, con éxito, al estableci-

chivo, esgrimido repetidamente para negar el retorno de los documentos, por cuanto se trata de una unidad artificiosa que rompió la unidad de origen.

El director del Arxiu Nacional de Catalunya, Sants Lliurat, por su parte, se refirió a la historia de la reclamación documental que ha provocado un total de 57 intervenciones, interpelaciones, preguntas y proposiciones no de ley en los parlamentos catalán y español.

La situación de los documentos se halla en la actualidad pendiente del infor-

---

The Dignity Commission logo designed by Josep Companys, great nephew of Catalan President Lluís Companys who was executed on Franco's orders in 1940.

Intellectuals from all over the world sign in support of the return of what some termed the «Salamanca blood papers» (*La Vanguardia*. 12/6/2002).

Former catalan prime minister, Artur Mas, receives the book containing the 700 signatures of international professors in support for the Dignity Commission's demands, in the presence of Toni Strubell*, Julià Garcia*, Elisenda Romeu*, Josep Camps*, Carme Carmona* and the Catalan Government's director general of Cultural Heritage, Marc Meyer (21/6/2002. Photograph Esteve Fermí).

Josep Cruanyes* and Josep Maria Sans Travé (director of the Catalan National Archive) call for the return of the «Salamanca Papers» at the UCE summer university at Prada. (22/8/2002. UCE Photograph).

---

* The asterisk identifies members of the Dignity Commission Secretariat.

Carles Fontserè, victim
of the Francoist
pillaging, before a
wartime poster of his at
his home in Porqueres
(Photograph by Agustí
Ensesa, *La Vanguardia*).

Josep Maria Àlvarez, secretary
general of the UGT union, on
the way to Salamanca to
demand the return of UGT's
archives (14/10/2002.
Photograph Ivan Costa, *El
Triangle*).

Campaigners in the streets of Salamanca, carrying a laurel wreath to the Salamanca Archive in honour of all those who died through Franco's repression (14/10/2002. Photograph by Félix Corchado).

Aurora Fontoba, violinist from the «Franja de Ponent» region, plays the traditional Catalan song «El Cant dels Ocells» which Pau Casals had made famous, before the Salamanca Archive, with Carles Fontserè, Josep M. Andreu, Claudi Romeu* and Imma Albó*. (14/10/1002. Photograph by Ignasi Aragay, *Avui*).

Enric Borràs, spokesman of the Dignity Commission, vigourously addressing a rally before the Spanish Government's delegation office in Barcelona (15/10/2002. Photograph by Rafel Tixé).

Salvador Arderiu* reads out a letter addressed to president Aznar calling for the return of the Papers. Pla de Palau (15/10/2002. Photograph by Rafel Tixé).

A large crowd demand the return of the «Salamanca Papers» in the Plaça del Rei (15/10/2002. Photograph by Rafel Tixé).

Actor Joel Joan presents the meeting «Against the darkness of Francoism» which called for the «Papers» (15/10/2002. Photograph by Rafel Tixé).

Distinguished Catalan writer Teresa Pàmies reads the Commission Manifesto (15/10/2002. Photograph by Rafel Tixé).

Raimon sings «Diguem no!» in answer to the forceful retention of the «Papers» in Salamanca (15.10.2002. Photograph by Rafel Tixé).

Toni Strubell, coordinator of the Dignity Commission, delivers the final speech at the memorable meeting (15/10/2002. Photograph by Rafel Tixé).

Campaigners protest about the opening of the «Propaganda en Guerra» exhibition in Salamanca. Mariona Companys (great niece of Lluís Companys, Catalan president executed in 1940), Elisenda Romeu*, Joaquim Ferrer*, Josep Guia*, Carles Bonet, Josep Altayó*, Marta Rojals*, Josep Maria Goñi and Rosa Maria Carrasco, with local support group members (12/11/2002).

A cartoon by Fer (28/5/2004. *Avui* newspaper) throws light on the ideology of some of those who defend the Salamanca Archive.

A presentation of the Dignity Commission in Lleida, organised by Òmnium Cultural (25/10/2002. Photograph by Marc Garrofé, *La Mañana*).

Pep Guia* and Paula Martínez Ros* present the Dignity Commission in the Main Hall of Valencia University (26/11/2002. Photograph by M. Lorenzo).

An emotive tribute paid to Salamanca «heroes», councillor Teresa Carvajal and suspended journalist Aníbal Lozano, with Jordi Porta and Toni Strubell*, at the Barcelona Atheneum Club (22/5/2003. Photograph by Cristina Calderé, *Avui*).

Emeritus Professor Henry Ettinghausen receives a tribute in Barcelona for his generous service in favour of the Dignity Commission (19/12/2003. Photograph by Rafel Tixé).

Prize-winning British-born Catalan novelist Matthew Tree amusingly compares the excesses of Franco to those of Margaret Thatcher against the miners. Tribute to Ettinghausen (19/12/2003. Photograph by Rafel Tixé).

Carles Fontserè at the Ettinghausen tribute, with Montserrat Milian*, compère at the event and the Ettinghausen family (19/12/2003. Photograph by Rafel Tixé).

Professor Til Stegmann, from Frankfurt University, another staunch supporter of the Dignity Commission, at the Farinera del Clot, with Imma Albó* and Josep Camps*. (19.12.2003. Photograph by Rafel Tixé).

Josep Cruanyes* in Lleida with a group of mayors, drawing up plans for legal action regarding the recovery of local municipal archives from Salamanca (13/1/2004. Photograph by Toni Alcàntara, *La Mañana*).

Argentinian Nobel Peace Prize-winner, Adolfo Pérez Esquivel, with Toni Strubell* and Josep Cruanyes*, at the Barcelona Fòrum (13/4/2004. Photograph by Pere Virgili, *Avui*).

Cartoon by Lluís Puyal on the Archive case, an image that the party Izquierda Castellana pasted all over Salamanca in 2004.

Jordi Porta, Henry Ettinghausen, Joan Rigol (president of the Dignity Commission support groups), Toni Strubell* and Aurora Fontoba appeal to president Rodríguez Zapatero to return the documents. Barcelona Journalist Collegiate Association (29/4/2004. Photograph by Rafel Tixé).

The official Dignity Commission party after a meeting with the minister of Culture, Ms Carmen Calvo, before the Ministry in Madrid. (Josep Cruanyes*, Joan Boadas (AAC), José Luis de las Heras, Pep Guia*, Ximo Puig, Joan Rigol, Heribert Barrera, Jordi Font, Enric Borràs*, and Toni Strubell*. Madrid, 26/5/2004).

Pep Guia*, Salamanca University's José Luis de las Heras, Josep Cruanyes* and Enric Borràs* campaigning for the return of the documents in Madrid (26/5/2004).

The campaign reaches the football grounds. FC Terrassa's main stand on June 5 2004 during the match against UD Salamanca the banner reads "we want the Catalan papers held in Salamanca" (Photograph by Mané Espinosa, *La Vanguardia*).

The campaign was also reflected on walls around the country such as this one near Llagostera in northern Catalonia.

Dignity Commission party after a meeting with the Catalan Culture Minister, Ms Caterina Mieras, before the Conselleria in Barcelona. Emília Capell (Vice-President of the AAC), Josep Cruanyes*, Odina Capo, Enric Borràs* and Toni Strubell* (28/6/2004).

The second meeting of the Dignity Comission was held on 11 February, again at the Ateneu Barcelonès. This time the main conference hall was to be used as there was a significant increase in the attendance. Many new associations and bodies now sought representation on the Dignity Commission. This meeting was to prove significant for two major reasons: firstly, because more information was now available on the exhibition that was to be held in Salamanca. It had been disclosed that the exhibition was to bear the name «Propaganda in time of war», and that it was to open on 5 October, remaining open to the public until 22 January. It was revealed that it was to show materials held in The Civil War Archive in Salamanca, the institution where Catalan and other Republican documents had been retained since their initial spoliation.

By spring 2002, the Dignity Commission had become a considerable landmark in Catalan society. At the end of the year it would be rated as one of the leading and most influential social groups in the Catalan Countries by Catalan internet newspaper «Vilaweb». The Commission was to engage in a whole range of activities aimed at recovering Catalan documents retained in Salamanca. One of the most outstanding of these activities was to be the international support campaign run in the summer of 2002. There was also to be attendance at four meetings held in Salamanca — two of which involved special charter flights — official receptions both at the seat of the Catalan Government — at the Generalitat Palace — and at the seat of the Catalan Parliament, meetings at the major Catalan universities[2] and at the Ministry of Culture — May 2004 — as well as one with Catalan Culture minister, Ms Caterina Mieras, in June 2004. Meetings and talks all around the country have been very numerous between early 2002 and September 2004.

---

2. Universitat de València, Universitat de Barcelona, Universitat Catalana d'Estiu, etc.

The Office in Valencia

> On the last Sunday of October:
> the way is well known,
> let's make for the road
> and gather at El Puig.

These are the first lyrics of the famous 'Al Tall' song that calls on all those who love their land and nation to attend the El Puig rally in October. Those attending the meeting at the Muntanyeta del Castell in October 2002, were to hear the Dignity Commission's presentation given by its Coordinator, Toni Strubell, who had also been guest speaker at the most important of Valencian cultural prize-giving ceremonies the night before, that of the «Premis Octubre». At the popular El Puig rally, the final details regarding the creation of the Commission's Office in Valencia were decided in a conversation between Toni Strubell, Enric Borràs and Josep Guia, and the question of who the ideal person would be to do the job was discussed. All provisional arrangements were later ratified by the Secretariat.

The question had already been raised the day before at a meeting between Dignity Commission members and Eliseu Climent and Antoni Gisbert of Acció Cultural del País Valencià (ACPV), a prestigious cultural organisation that was to be asked to accommodate the new office of the Dignity Commission in Valencia. It had also been decided that the Commission would pay the fees of the person running the office. ACPV had previously announced its public support for the Dignity Commission at a press conference held on 18 October 2002, at which the press received copies of a letter sent by the organisation to the President of the Valencian Government, requesting his participation in the call for the return of Valencian documents held at Salamanca. In the 30 July edition of the weekly *El Temps* (edition 946), Josep Cruanyes had published an article under the title «El segrest dels documents del País Valencià» («The seizure of documents in Valencia»), which summarized confiscation operations by Franco's men in Valencia in 1938-1939. In edition number 958 of the same magazine, on 22 October 2002, Núria Cadenas published a long report on the activities of the Dignity Commission.

The establishment of the Dignity Commission in Valencia in October 2002 may be viewed as a direct consequence of the participation of some of its members in the Catalan Summer University held in August at Prada de

Conflent, as well as at the massive rally held in Barcelona's Passeig de Lluís Companys on the 11 September (National Day), where Toni Strubell was to speak. These events led one of the local socialist parties — PSAN — and ACPV to invite Commission members to Valencia.

The day after the El Puig meeting, Josep Guia offered the post of secretary of the Dignity Commission's office in Valencia to Paula Martínez Ros. The proposal was accepted by the Secretariat and on 30 October Josep Guia and Paula Martínez were to attend the next Dignity Commission Secretariat meeting in Barcelona. The new office of the Dignity Commission in Valencia was to open on 4 November 2002.

Activities carried out so far

The activities carried out so far in Valencia have had a dual purpose: firstly, to make known the existence of Valencian documents withheld at Salamanca; and secondly, to encourage all kinds of organisations and individuals to strengthen the call for their repatriation. With these objectives in mind, members have participated in many meetings since the Dignity Commission's initial presentation at the University of Valencia on 26 November 2002.

As regards contacts with associations and political parties, on 13 November 2002 an initial information session was held with members of the parties BNV, Esquerra Valenciana, PSAN, EUPV, Esquerra Verda and ERPV, and productive meetings have been held with Joaquim Puig (PSPV-PSOE) and Dolors Pérez (EUPV), members of the Valencian Parliament. Parties involved in all these meetings have been very receptive to be the idea of co-operating in the recovery of the Valencian documents and have shown their support for the Dignity Commission. Especially interesting was the bill presented by Joan Francesc Peris, with the support of all left-wing groups, in the Valencian Parliament.

As regards the position taken by the political parties, mention must be made of the debate organised by the Association of Valencian Archivists on 11 December 2002, as part of the Association's Second Conference. The session was chaired by the Association's secretary, and the following participated in it: Valencian MPs David Serra (PP), Francesc Colomer (PSPV-PSOE), Dolors Pérez (EUPV) and Joan Francesc Peris (Esquerra Verda). Also present was José Luis Villacañas, Director General of the Valencian Government's Book Department. At the debate,

Peris, Pérez and Colomer spoke in support of the repatriation of the documents, granting credit to the technical argument based on the principle of origin and the law of heritage. The also resorted to political arguments such as the need to remedy the shortcomings of the Transición period, the possibility of recovering collective history and the need to connect with Salamanca's own idea of returning material taken from America and to apply it to the papers stolen by Franco. In answer to this, Serra and Villacañas did little more that repeat Spanish Government justificactions to explain why «archive unity» had to be maintained and claimed there was still not enough public demand for the papers' return.

Besides political organisations, other cultural groups have shown their support for the cause. At its AGM on 23 November 2002, the Federation of Local Studies Institutes of Valencia (FIECOV) decided to ask the Valencian Government to request the return of the seized documents to their rightful owners. The Els Ports Local Studies Centre also showed its support in a letter addressed to the Valencian Office of the Dignity Commission, a gesture that shows how well-received the Commission was becoming.

From the moment the Valencian Office of the Dignity Commission opened, it was a priority to contact Valencian town and city halls. The motion that had already been used in Catalonia was amended and sent to the councillors who had taken an interest in the issue.

Motions have been presented to councils and many of them have been carried, in some cases with the favourable votes of PP members, although, in general, the motions were largely carried in councils with a left-wing and/or nationalist majority. However, many local politicians to this day are unaware that their communities were the victims of mass document pillaging.

The documents stolen

Not knowing exactly what documents a particular institution such as a town council may claim back from Salamanca is one of the aspects that makes the process more difficult, not so much because of the political demand as such, but because of the difficulty in knowing how to stipulate the demand in administrative and legal terms. At present we do not have a complete list of the public or private bodies that may be considered direct victims of thefts.

At the outset, we only had information supplied by Josep Cruanyes on forty-four Valencian municipalities with documents in Salamanca. Subsequently, as a result of the visit made to the Salamanca Archive on 12 November 2002, we were able to draw up an additional list of towns in the Castelló area, and also had access to the book *Documentación sobre la Guerra Civil en Alicante. Inventario de la serie político-social de Alicante. Archivo Histórico Nacional sección Guerra Civil* published by the Gil-Albert Institute (Alacant Pronvicial Council) in 1983, featuring a study by Maria Teresa Díez de los Ríos. This allowed us to extend the list of affected towns to one hundred and fifty seven. More recently, we have also had access to the *Guía de la Documentación Valenciana existente en el Archivo Histórico Nacional sección Guerra Civil*, compiled by Emma Jávega Charco. This work enabled us to extend our list to over two hundred towns, although we still feel that it is too early to give a final figure. This is the provisional list:

Ademús, Adsúbia, Agost, Agres, Aigües, Aiora, Alacant, Alaquàs, Albaida, Alberic, Albocàsser, Alcalà de Xivert, Alcàsser, Alcoi, l'Alcora, Algemesí, Alginet, l'Alguenya, Almassora, Almenara, Almoradí, l'Alqueria de la Comtessa, les Alqueries de la Plana, Altea, Alzira, Ares, Asp, Banyeres de Mariola, Bellreguard, Benasau, Benasal, Beneixama, Benejússer, Beniarbeig, Beniarjó, Beniarrés, Benicarló, Benicàssim, Benidorm, Benifaió, Benigànim, Benilloba, Benillup, Benimodo, Benirredrà, Benissa, Benissanó, Benitatxell, Biar, Bicorb, Bocairent, Bolulla, Borriana, Borriol, Bugarra, Busot, Cabanes de l'Arc, Càlig, Calles, Callosa d'En Sarrià, Callosa de Segura, Calp, el Camp de Mirra, Canet lo Roig, Carcaixent, Carlet, les Casas Bajas, Castalla, Castell de Cabres, Castell de Castells, Castelló de la Plana, Caudiel, Cinctorres, Cocentaina, Cortes d'Arenós, les Coves de Vinromà, Coix, Crevillent, Culla, Daia Nova, Dénia, Dolores, Elda, Elx, Ènguera, Eslida, Fanzara, Figueres, Figueroles d'Alcalatén o de Domenjó, Finestrat, Fondó de les Neus, Formentera de Segura, Gandia, Gavarda, Godella, Guardamar, Ibi, Llanera de Ranes, Llíria, Llucena, Lludient, Manises, Moncofa, Monòver, Montesa, Montfort, Morella, Muro d'Alcoi, Mutxamel, Novelda, la Nucia, Nules, Oliva, l'Olleria, Onda, Ondara, Onil, Ontinyent, Orba, Oriola, Orpesa, l'Orxa, Orxeta, Parcent, Paterna, Pedreguer, Pego, Petrer, el Pinós de Monòver, Pobla d'Arenós, Pobla Llarga, la Pobla Tornesa, la Pobla del Duc, Polinyà del Xúquer, Polop, el Puig, Quart de Poblet, Ràfol, el Ràfol d'Almúnia, Redovà, Relleu, Requena, Ribesalbes, Rocafort, Rojals, la Romana, Rossell, Sagunt, Salem, les Salines d'Elda, Saix, Sant Joan de

Moro, Sant Rafel del Riu, Sant Vicent del Raspeig, Santa Pola, Serra d'En Galceran, Sogorb, Sollana, Sueca, Tales, Tavernes Blanques, Tibi, Torre Baixa, Torreblanca, la Torre de les Maçanes, Torrent, Torrevella, Traiguera, les Useres, València, la Vall d'Alba, el Verger, Vilafamés, Vilafranca, la Vila Joiosa, Vilanova d'Alcolea, Vila-real, la Vilavella, el Villar de l'Arquebisbe, Villena, Vinaròs, Xàbia, Xacarella, Xàtiva, Xelva, Xiva, Xiva de Morella, Xixona.

Other confiscated materials are very diverse. They range from posters by Josep Renau or Artur Ballester to war photographs taken in Valencia by Deschamps or Kati Horna, postcards by V. Ballester Marco or Vorin, political pamphlets, periodicals such as *Fragua Social, Portavoz de la CNT, Adelante, Diario Socialista de la mañana, Amanecer Rojo. Semanario de la Juventud* o *Heraldo de Castellón, Diario del Frente Popular*; books of minutes from masonic lodges such as Libre Examen from Alcoi, Sol Naciente from Vila-real or Librepensadores from Valencia; reports sent from active units on the front line; documents relating to parties and unions, etc. There are also private papers such as letters sent by soldiers, certificates and wills, etc.

To visit the Archive in search of documents is both a thrilling and moving experience. One does not always find what one is looking for, because some boxes are misleadingly labelled. However, even when distracted from one's initial search, it is always compelling to uncover fragments of lives affected by a cruel war. This experience should be possible for us Valencians in our own homeland, the place where the events happened and where the documents originated. It is here that there is greater need to discover the details of our past.

The echo in the media

From the outset, the demand for the return of the Valencian documents held at Salamanca has found positive response. The press conference organised by ACPV on 18 October 2002 attracted the attention of Valencian newspapers, which all gave wide coverage to the issue. Amongst other things, they took a special interest in the part played in the confiscations by several significant Francoist collaborators such as Adolfo Rincón de Arellano, who went on to become Mayor of Valencia, and Miquel Adlert, who was later one of the main promoters of Valencian linguistic secessionism with regard to Catalan (i.e. claiming Valencian to be a language different to Catalan).

From then on, there has been a regular flow of news in relation to the documents and Ràdio Nou (Valencian Public Radio) and TV3 (Catalan Public TV) have broadcast several short interviews on the issue. When the Dignity Commission made its first presentation at the University of Valencia, the University weekly *Nou Disè* reported it in detail, making it headline news and dedicating a full page to the issue inside.

Future prospects

The public impact of the demands for the return of the confiscated documents is still far from strong. This means that the activities outlined above will have to continue for some time until we find ourselves in a more favourable political situation. Nevertheless, the hard line taken by the former Spanish government will surely become less extreme when, through the courts, private individuals and legal entities begin to prove their ownership of particular documents and retrieve them.

As mentioned above, however, the difficulty here lies in determining which documents each private individual and institution can claim. A collective and non-defined claim would be unacceptable before the law, yet it is as yet difficult to compile a detailed list of what belongings were seized; moreover, there is a risk that any list drawn up would be incomplete. Besides ensuring publicity, support, and political statements, it will be necessary to assemble a catalogue of the documents being claimed. Whatever happens, it is our job to make sure the question remains open for discussion and that it keeps in the news until the documents are retrieved.

International support for the Commission

From the time of its creation in January 2002, the Dignity Commission has had two overriding beliefs: 1) to achieve the return of the «Salamanca Papers», the role of the mass media would be crucial. 2) to cause an impact on the mass media — and hence Catalan public opinion — it would be necessary to resort to new strategies. From day one, the strategy that was adopted was to be based on avoiding «classical» campaign styles and on searching for more effective and ambitious methods: that of a campaign based on international support.

The main objective was to draw up an International Manifesto (Declaració Internacional) which could receive the support of personalities from all over the world, especially from the academic world and universities. Legitimacy for the cause would be sought with the endorsement of people with academic solvency. Over the course of Spring 2002, a team of people, under the auspices of the Dignity Commission, started to look for support for the campaign. The following Manifesto was sent to personalities and academics to gain their support.

Support for the Dignity Commission

The signatories of this Declaration — university academics of different disciplines — have been informed about the fact that the Salamanca Civil War Archive is largely made up of documents accumulated by the State Office for the Recovery of Documents Office, an entity set up by military dictator General Franco for the seizure of materials obtained in a selective fashion during and after the Civil War and which were to be one of the main sources of information used in an unprecedented wave of repression against democrats in «special courts» as of 1940.

We are also aware that at the Salamanca European Culture City 2002 festivities, the organising body has programmed an exhibition of «War Propaganda» between 5 October and 22 December, in which part of these documents are to go on show, without any form of permission nor consent from the rightful owners of these papers (the Catalan Government, Catalan City Halls, Unions, Political Parties, private individuals etc.).

Given that the Spanish Government ratified (9 June 1960) the The Hague International Agreement on the Protection of Cultural Goods in the Event of Armed Conflict (14 May 1954), which decrees the immunity of goods and the duty that binds holders to protect them from any form of forceful requisition or appropiation, resulting from international conflicts or not.

Given that UNESCO's International Archives Council has repeatedly stated that legitimate owners have the right to recover documents that have been taken as war spoil or stolen during an armed conflict (Resolution 46/10 of UNO's 1991 General Assembly).

And given that from 1978 until today, the elected representatives of the Catalan people and the Catalan Parliament itself have unanimously voted (Resolution of 18 May 1989) and repeatedly demanded the return of the stolen documents — both public and private — we believe it to be in our full right to give our support to the Dignity Commission in its campaign and to urge the Spanish authorities to:

— Fulfil, without further delay, the agreement taken by the Spanish Government's cabinet (15 March 1995) which orders the return of the documents.

— Suspend and withdraw from the Salamanca 2002 programme the exhibition «Propaganda en Guerra» (War Propaganda) if it fails to have the explicit permission of the Catalan authorities.

To head the list, the Secretariat of the Dignity Commission thought that it would be a good idea to unite a series of names of people that might act as a reference for academic, political and social circles. These names could serve to bestow prestige on the cause and help the campaign to attract more attention. The list, that was to become longer as the days went by, gained the support of the following personalities, amongst which two ex-Heads of State and two Nobel Peace Prize winners are to be found:

Hebe Bonafini, (President of Argentina's Madres de la Plaza de Mayo), David Cardús (Professor of Medicine at Texas Bates University), Noam Chomsky (Professor at MIT), Francesco Cossiga (Emeritus President of Italy), Françoise David (President of the Federation of Quebecois Women), Peter Gabriel (musician), Baroness Gloria Hooper (Member of the House of Lords), Federico Mayor Zaragoza (Ex-Secretary General of UNESCO), Rigoberta Menchú (Nobel Peace Prize winner), Danielle Mitterand (President France Libertés), Georges Moustaki (musician), Joan Oró (NASA scientist), Sgouridis Panagioty (Vice-President of the Greek Parliament), Adolfo Pérez Esquivel (Nobel Peace Prize winners), James Petras (Professor at Binghampton), Paul Preston, (Professor at LSE), Joan Rigol (President of the Catalan Parliament), Nawal El Saadawi (Egyptian writer), Mario Soares (Ex-President of Portugal), Mikis Theodrakis (musician), Virginia Tsouderos (ex-Deputy Foreign Minister of Greece), Howard Zinn (Emeritus Professor Boston University).

When the news of this international support came out, the shock wave in the mass media was tidal, not only in Catalonia, but throughout the State and even beyond. One American journalist would describe the campaign *as* «the most important effort to put the Catalan cause on the world map in 25 years». The scenario chosen for the presentation of the Manifesto was the main hall of the Barcelona Central University in a cerimony chaired by University Dean, Joan Tugores. Representatives of the families affected by the robberies and representatives of the principal parties likewise affected — those giving support to the Dignity Commission — were all present. Those addressing the sizeable audience were to be Toni Strubell, coordinator of the Dignity Comission, the Catalan Government's Director General for the Heritage, Marc Mayer, the historian and pioneer of historians' journeys to Salamanca, Anscari Mundó, and the Emeritus Professor of Southampton University, Dr. Henry Ettinghausen.

Even mass media that are normally not too partial to an excessively pro-Catalan view of things were obliged to give extensive reports on the event. *La Vanguardia*, for example, placed a red headline (above the main headline) on its front page with the news: «Manifiesto mundial por los "Papeles de Salamanca".»[3] On page 40 there were photographs of Noam Chomsky, Paul Preston, Mario Soares and Peter Gabriel next to a report signed by the prestigious cultural life journalist, Josep Maria Sòria. It was headed: «Intelectuales de todo el mundo exigen el retorno de los "Papeles de Salamanca".»[4] *El País* gave less space to the news, although a report appeared under the headline: «500 personalities from 47 countries support the return of the «Salamanca Papers»» on June 12 2002 In the Catalan press the news was also to get first-page treatment and the first full page of «Culture» in *Avui* had the headline: «World support for the return of the "Salamanca papers".» The news was illustrated with photographs of five of the signatories: Rigoberta Menchú, Adolfo Pérez Esquivel — both Nobel Peace Prize-winners — Noam Chomsky, singer Peter Gabriel and Danielle Mitterrand. Apart from actually signing their support for the Manifesto, many international signatories also sent messages of support to the Dignity Commission in the following weeks. Here is a sample of them:

> It is important that the «Salamanca Papers» should be returned to the people. Memory is the history and life of peoples. It is necessary, both for the present and for the future, that the events lived in Spain be evaluated and known. I send you fraternal greetings of Peace and Goodwill.
>
> Adolfo Pérez Esquivel
> Holder of the Nobel Peace Prize, Argentina

> Thank you for your invitation. It is with pride that I sign your petition. Looking forward to meeting you in Barcelona.
>
> Francesco Cossiga
> President Emeritus and Life Senator of Italy

> I should like to take this opportunity to show my appreciation of this important initiative that the Dignity Commission is undertaking with a view to recovering important historical documents that disappeared from Catalonia during the Franco dictatorship.
>
> Mario Soares
> former President of Portugal

---

3. World Manifesto for the «Salamanca Papers».
4. «Intellectuals from all over the World demand the return of the «Salamanca Papers».» See photograph section.

In the name of Rigoberta Menchú, President of our Foundation, we wish to show our commitment by joining you in the noble aim of restoring such an important and painful part of the history of Spain to its lawful owners: the victims. For our part, in the light of the struggle for justice in the face of the Guatemalan genocide, we have decided to set up a major centre for the documentation of Historical Memory in all instances in which the tragedy lived by different peoples can be recorded and preserved so that the truth and the justice of the victims' cause may be vindicated and proper legal evidence provided for trials for crimes against humanity under international law. You may therefore count on the personal and institutional support of the Rigoberta Menchú Tum Foundation for the campaign to have the «Blood Papers» returned.

Alfonso Alem Rojo
Executive Director, Fundación Rigoberta Menchú Tum

To keep the Catalan papers in the Salamanca archive is not just a crime against history but an insult to the victims of fascism. I give all my support to those who are working to achieve their return to the Catalan archives from which they should never have been taken.

Noam Chomsky
Professor at the Massachussets Institute of Technology

First of all, I wish to express my support for the movement to have returned to Catalonia the Catalan papers held in the Salamanca archive. The materials now kept in Salamanca were plundered and scrutinised by people who were looking for «evidence» of crimes, such as membership of left-wing, freemason, Catalan nationalist, or simply democratic, organisations. These archives constitute the data base that made possible the repression carried out in the 1940s under the infamous Law for the Repression of Freemasonry and Communism. The fact that the Salamanca archive has not returned these papers to their rightful owners can only be described as scandalous. The argument on which this is based is that they now form part of an important archive. However, why on earth cannot the originals be given back and copies made in order to preserve the integrity of the archive? That would have been the most proper and democratic thing to do, and 25 years have gone by in which that could have been done.

Paul Preston
Professor of History, London School of Economics

Pleased to send my whole-hearted support to this worthy cause, though I am no academic, but merely an elderly researcher for a Scottish National Party Member of the Scottish Parliament. I am based in Oban in the Western

Highlands of Scotland and was a first-time visitor to Catalonia and Barcelona last year.

Kenneth McColl
Researcher, Ayrshire, Scotland

I support this campaign, for what I understand from your message to be the
reasons.

Thomas N. Bisson
Professor, Harvard University, USA

I fully support the efforts of the Dignity Commission and the UNESCO
Centre in Barcelona to recover the documents taken by Franco's army in
1939, and not yet returned to their rightful owners: the Archives of the
Catalan Government, University Libraries, Trade Unions, political groups
etc.

François-Pierre Gingras
Professor, Université d'Ottawa, Canada

From my point of view, these documents form an integral part of Catalan
history. Therefore, it would be more than reasonable that these documents
be returned to Catalonia so that they can be given á place in one of the
archives or museums of Catalonia.

Auke van der Goot
Civil Servant, Ministry of the Interior, The Netherlands

I sent the message to all American scholars that I know who care about
Catalan affairs. I hope that helps. Good luck with your campaign and
thanks very much for doing this. You should be given the Cross of St
George!

Martina Milla Bernad
Lecturer, Emory University, USA

I want to make public my support for the efforts being made by the Catalans
to recover the «Salamanca Papers».

Thomas Harrington
Assistant Professor, Trinity College, Hartford, USA

I am sending this message to give my support to the campaign that fights to
have the documents belonging to the Generalitat de Catalunya returned to
their rightful owner by the Spanish Government.

Cristina Sanz
Associate Professor, Georgetown University, USA

I would like to lend my support to the Dignity Commission's attempt to repatriate Catalan public records plundered by the Franco regime. At this late date, it is inexcusable for the Spanish authorities to continue hoarding public property stolen by the fascists. The fact that these records were used to repress and butcher representatives of a legitimate democratic government should further give pause.

Jan Reinhart
Library Manager, Rutgers University, USA

It is completely unacceptable for a democratic Spanish government worthy of the name to retain as war booty documents belonging to the autonomous government of Catalonia. To include them in an exhibit of «war propaganda» is insulting to the memory of Catalans who died in defense of the Republic, and to the many who were forced into exile or suffered reprisals at the hands of the Franco regime. Such uses of these documents continue the Spanish Civil War into the present, and prevent the completion of the transition to democracy.

Susan DiGiacomo
Assistant Professor, Amhurst College, USA

I send you my deepest support and solidarity in your cause. I wish you lots of success!

Silvana Piga
Archivist, Universidad de San Andrés, Argentina

A curse on those who rob people of their memory! Condemned be those who in their hypocrisy continue to enjoy the fruits that Fascism extracted from our lacerated flesh! In solidarity, from a country that knows why it is suffering.

Jorge Rodolfo Busch
Engineer, Universidad de Buenos Aires, Argentina

An archive is an important research tool, and I fully support your desire to see it return to Catalonia!

Daniel Pfeiffer
Computer Scientist, Université Pau Sabatier, Toulouse, France

As I have the war experience (as a citizen, not as a soldier!) from the former Yugoslavia (I'm Croatian), similar misuses are well known to me. They were done from all three (or four) sides of the former «Yu» conflict, and are, in fact, still at work. Years are needed for such a things to be corrected, souls to be satisfied. But it would never work without constant pressure on the governments and organisations to clear the things. That's why I strongly support such efforts. The victims have a right at least to this last act of dignity made in their honour: that the truth is presented. As the truth is, especially in wartime, a very elastic word, it is up to the community of the victims, and not the torturers and murderers, to decide what to do with the documents. What would happen if the Auschwitz and similar documents were left to Germans and Austrians to handle?

Miljenko Cemeljic
Lecturer, Universität Potsdam, Germany

I would be delighted to support the campaign, but would like to ask you to consider the extension of the campaign to include all treasures that were plundered from a huge number of countries during various periods of invasion, colonisation and exploitation. A huge number of treasures that we removed from South Africa sit in Europe, particularly. Egypt's archaeological sites have been plundered for centuries to stock European and American museums and private collections, as no doubt is the case in South America. Few of these countries have the power to create a strong enough voice to demand what is theirs back. The extension of your campaign will add voice to this.

Brian Garman
Lecturer, Rhodes University, South Africa

From what you have told me of the case of the Salamanca Blood Papers and the campaign that has been organised for their return to Catalonia from Salamanca and the work of the Dignity Commission, I would tend to agree that documents stolen by Franco's army in 1939 be returned to their rightful owners: the Catalan Government. I hope this message can assist in advancing the cause.

Robin Palmer
Associate Professor, Rhodes University, South Africa

I do wholeheartedly support your efforts to get the papers back and placed in a properly constituted archive.

Kay McCormick
Associate Professor, University of Cape Town, South Africa

I give my full support to your case. It is deplorable that these very important documents have not been returned. Please inform me of the ways in which I can make my voice count.

Nelia Saxby
Professor, University of Cape Town, South Africa

I am very happy to add my name in strong support of this campaign, the goals of which I share completely.

David Blackbourn
Professor, Harvard University, USA

I wish to support your case-we in South Africa know what it means to go through a process of democratization. Good luck!

Piet Erasmus
Professor, University of the Free State, South Africa

I wish to express my solidarity with your campaign. As an Argentine citizen, I cannot fail to remember the suffering and pain suffered by thousands of Republicans who went into exile in my country. Over the years, thousands Catalan militants have made invaluable contributions to the struggle of the people in Argentina. The campaign to recover the documents and to reconstruct the memory of the people in Spain and in Catalonia is the struggle of all those who fight, as did our comrades in the 1930s in Argentina, in Europe and in every continent, for a world that is different, possible and necessary.

Emilio Horacio Taddei
Latin American Council for Social Sciences, Buenos Aires, Argentina

I wish to urge the return of the Catalan papers, now constituting archival material, taken at the end of the Civil War, to their rightful owners.

Dr. Nathaniel Smith
Franklin and Marshall College, Lancaster, USA

I was unaware of the business that you have explained to me, but I am very happy to add my support to your appeal. I simply do not see why the Catalan documents should not be returned to Catalonia.

Maurizio Punzo
Professor, Università degli Studi di Milano, Italy

I hereby declare that, if UNESCO regulations have been infringed, I fully support the demands of the Dignity Commission for the so-called «Blood Papers» to be returned to their original archives. At the same time, I must say that I disagree both with the perpetuation of a spirit of conflict that confuses 2002 with 1950 which Madrid expresses in a rhetoric that presumes to treat Catalonia like a rebel province and which Catalonia expresses in a Catalan nationalist discourse that presumes to treat Spain like a foreign country that sent its troops in to occupy the Catalan lands.

Hans-Ingo Radatz
Associate Professor, Katholische Universität Eichstätt, Germany

I wish you success in the return of the papers in what appears to be a terrible case of injustice which has been allowed to persist.

Ralph Summy
Consultant, University of Queensland, Australia

I back you very willingly. It is not just a question of rational scientific research, but also of respect for history and for the political and cultural roots of the citizens of Catalonia. Please keep me informed.

Dr. Giuliana Laschi
Università degli Studi di Milano, Italy

I support your request to bring these stolen archives back. I consider the government's plans not to bring these archives back to the legitimate owners and to use them for its own purposes as an intolerable offense to democracy in general and to the democratic strivings of the Spanish peoples and their researchers in particular.

Alf Johansson
Professor, Oslo University, Norway

I received your appeal from the Dignity Commission and I back your call for the return of these documents. Failure to return them would mean perpetuating Francoist practices.

Tahar Mansouri
Professor, Université de Mannouba, Tunis, Tunisia

I support your request to bring these stolen archives back. I consider the government's plans to not bring these archives back to the legitimate owners and to use them for its own purposes as an intolerable offense to democracy in general and to the democratic strivings of the Spanish people's and their I very much support your campaign. You might find it helpful to get in touch with the University of Iceland. It and the Icelandic government fought a similar battle with the Danes in the 1950s and 60s for the return of manuscripts that were taken to Denmark during the colonial period. Iceland won the debate and all the manuscripts were returned home.

Dr. Astvaldur Astvaldsson
Lecturer, University of Liverpool, England

All the best in your efforts. We Greeks also want the marbles of the Parthenon back from UK.

Domna Pastourmatzi
Associate Professor, Aristotle University, Thessaloniki, Greece

Please add my name to your list/petition regarding these Catalan archival materials. Frankly, I am surprised that King Juan Carlos has not already seen to this outrageous abuse of authority. Now that that bastard Franco is dead, maybe my conscience will allow me to visit Spain!

Eric A. Arnold
Associate Professor, Denver University, USA

Please keep me informed of the campaign. Indeed, I feel strongly about this, since, in the early nineties, when I resided in Barcelona, I was forced to make the journey to Salamanca in order to consult this very archive.

Dr. Chris Ealham
Head of Studies, University of Wales, Cardiff, Wales

I would like to express my support. It is high time that these documents were returned to where they rightfully belong. I will pass this information on to my colleagues.

Dr. Caragh Wells
Lecturer, University of Bristol, England

We back the creation of the Dignity Commission with total conviction and hope that it will have the strength to attain its objectives. We express our solidarity and identity with you.

Nilda Tincopa Montoya
Defence Team & Peasant Consultancy, Organisation for the Defence of Human Rights, Peru

From the Truth and Reconciliation Commission of Peru, I salute the creation of the Dignity Commission and trust that the demands you have put forward will be met.

Viviana Valz Gen
The Truth Commission, Peru

Thank you for your mail about the Salamanca papers, of which I was quite ignorant. I wholeheartedly lend support to the Dignity Committee in their attempt to redress a palpable and long-standing injustice. I believe that the authorities should, without delay, return the archives to their rightful owners and submit an apology.

Richard A Cardwell
Professor, University of Nottingham, England

Please add my name to the list of those calling for the return of the Salamanca «Blood Papers». The return of these papers is of vital importance. It is a matter of justice; it is a matter of historical accuracy; it is a matter of preserving the truth for the future. I support your efforts whole-heartedly. Please let me know what else I may do to help.

Mark Leier
Associate Professor, Center for Labour Studies, Simon Fraser University, USA

I believe that it is the responsibility of government to preserve all official documents from the past. The responsibility is all the greater when documents have been politicized by being used for purposes for which they were never intended. The Catalan papers should be returned to Catalonia and made available for scholarly use.

Nicholas Canny
Professor, National University of Ireland, Galway, Ireland

I write, as requested, in support of the campaign for the return of the «Salamanca Papers». As a specialist in 20th-century Portugal, I feel particularly strongly that material of this type relating to this period of Iberian history should reside in its appropriate location with the greatest degree of access.

Dr. Norrie MacQueen
Head of Department, University of Dundee, Scotland

I am delighted to back the absolutely legitimate request for the return of the «Blood Papers» to Catalonia. They were stolen and criminally exploited. The Spanish government is under an obligation to redress this extremely grave injustice and, at the same time, to respect the autonomy of Catalonia as regards what it holds most precious: its culture, its past... its own archives.

Edmond Orban
Professor, Université de Montréal, Quebec

I wholeheartedly support the Dignity Commission and join academics throughout the world who are demanding that documents that were confiscated —and used to incarcerate, and in some cases assassinate, Spaniards who supported the legitimately created Republic— be returned to their rightful owners. It is an outrage that these documents are still under lock and key in Salamanca so many years after the end of the Franco Regime, since they suggest that the suppression of information continues to be a reality in Spain.

Shirley Mangini
Professor, California State University, USA

I think that the looting by the Spanish authorities of the Catalan documents held in Salamanca is unsurprising, although that does not make it any the less of an outrage. The syndrome of empire still rules the minds of the current Spanish government, which is in so many respects the heir of Francoism. Frustrated as it is by the total impossibility of regaining the hegemony it once enjoyed thanks to the silver stolen from America, it is only to be expected that it will do its best to rely on what remains of its right of conquest.

Josep Maria Murià
Director, Colegio de Jalisco, Guadalajara, Mexico

Thank you for sending me the texts on the stolen documents. As things are presented in them, I don't see how anybody could fail to support your case. The only thing I don't understand is, why do they (whoever it exactly is) refuse to return the papers to Catalonia? It seems to be a clear-cut case in every respect. Anyway, you have my support, if you think you are in need of a voice from Israel in this quite horrific time in our region.

Moshe Zuckermann
Professor, University of Tel Aviv, Israel

I hereby fully support the initiatives regarding the «Blood Papers». I hope that proper action will be taken, since culture — in the widest sense of the word — is the most precious thing mankind possesses!

Hans Keman
Professor, Universiteit Amsterdam, The Netherlands

I strongly support the case you are making. Access to the historical record is, I believe, a basic human right in any advanced democracy. I myself work on the East German secret police and have noted with grave disquiet that, since early March 2002, after a request from the German Government and former Chancellor Helmut Kohl, these archives which were open to scholars are now, to all intents and purposes, once again concealed from them. It is, therefore, important that those with the power to restrain access to the public record should be reminded about the serious consequences of their actions.

Anthony Glees
Professor, Brunel University, England

I declare my total support for the Dignity Commission's campaign to bring to public notice the case of the «Salamanca Papers» and to demand that the Spanish State return to us all the official documents of the Catalan Government that were looted in 1938 and 1939 and, what is more, used in order persecute, repress and imprison a great number of citizens, leading to the death of many of them. These papers should never have left Catalonia or, at the very least, they should have been returned as soon as democracy was restored. The fact that they were not returned then actually raises questions about the restoration of democracy.

Joan Sola Casadevall
Professor, Pennsylvania State University, USA

I add my protest to the many that have been made at the persistent failure of the current Spanish Government to return to Catalunya the archives that were plundered in Catalunya by Franco's Nationalist forces at the end of the Civil War and which were then used by the Franco dictatorship to oppress, persecute and even eliminate many who had sought to defend democracy against fascism.

Henry Ettinghausen
Professor Emeritus, University of Southampton, England

Please add my name to the list of academics urging the Spanish government to return the documents pillaged from Barcelona in 1939. As a lover of the city and its heroic past, I am glad to be included.

Christine Stansell
Professor, Princeton University, USA

I wish to express my complete support for your struggle to persuade the Spanish Government to return the documents that were pillaged in Barcelona in 1939 and never restored to their rightful owners. We want you to know that you are not alone and that we shall continue to accompany you in your just fight.

Manuel Ortega Hegg
Director of Casc, Universidad de Centroamérica, UCA, Nicaragua

You have my support for your petition. My parents are Civil War exiles.

Victoria L. Garcia
Lecturer, Princeton University, USA

I gladly subscribe your campaign against all tyrany. Franco was a tyrant. Other nations in Europe have done the same kind of pillaging. The Louvre and British Musem would be half empty if the stolen objects in them were to be returned from them.

Joxe Mallea-Olaetxe
Historian, University of Nevada, USA

Support from Spain

Sadly it has not been widespread practice in Spain to support Catalonia in its attempts to recover the Catalan documents withheld at Salamanca. Although it has not been a priority of the Dignity Commission to seek that support, in quantitative terms at least, it has been a question of some strategic importance throughout the Dignity Commission's campaign.

Traditionally, the solidarity of Spain with Catalonia has been a problematic question, and one that many may indeed consider to be a contradiction in terms. Some historians have even suggested that anti-Catalan feeling and thought are one of the pillars on which the nationalist ideology of some Spaniards seems to be built. With the same degree of logic articulated by the philosopher Ortega y Gasset in his intolerant belief in «conllevancia» — an attitude that nipped in the bud any petition for self-government so as to curb further calls and avoid the creation of precedents — the widely held view of many Spaniards as regards the «Salamanca Papers» could be summed up by saying «refuse them all and you will come out on top». This concept was parodied by Xavier Rupert de Ventós — Dignity Commission member, philisopher, ex EMP and writer — when he said the memorable phrase: «archive it all but you will not convince» (Salamanca, 15 October 2002), a statement which in turn reflects Miguel de Unamuno's 1936 utterance to the Francoists that «you will win but you will not convince», a phrase made in Salamanca itself.

Disregarding any scientific criteria regarding archive science, Spanish politicians of all walks have seen the controversy over the «Salamanca Papers» as a vote-winner that exploits the anti-Catalan feelings of large sections of their constituents, whose thinking may be influenced by the envy of regions suffering long-term economic depression (no fault of the Catalans, it must be pointed out), and who are unable to tackle the causes of their own age-old problems. For the local Castilian ruling class, the confiscation of documents that are of high symbolic value for the Catalan people seems to have become a policy that is seen as preferable to the articulation of policies aimed at restoring economical, industrial and demographical equilibrium between Spain's various autonomous communities.

Indeed the question of the «Salamanca Papers» has gone beyond a mere discussion of where some particular documents can best be stored. It has developed into a full scale dispute at state level. As far back as

1978, this became evident in the statements of Adolfo Suárez's Culture Minister, Ricardo de la Cierva, who went so far as to say that returning the Catalan archives would «break up the history of Spain». He added that it was «but a short step to breaking up Spain itself», dramatic words indeed! Seventeen years later, President Aznar was to resurrect that very same idea when he said that if the Catalan papers were returned from Salamanca, «the very Spanish nation would be placed in jeopardy». This is the apocalyptic attitude that has generally persisted in Spain's emotional reaction to Catalan demands. An instance of that reaction is the strident cry uttered to the crowds by leading Spanish writer and intellectual, Torrente Ballester, from the balcony of Salamanca town hall in 1995: the papers «are yours by right of conquest» he bellowed. It also includes a whole range of statements by mayors, regional and provincial presidents in Castile-León. Perhaps the instance many Catalans have considered the most insulting came in 1995 when the Socialist mayor of Salamanca, Sr. Málaga, ordered the main door of the old San Ambrosio building — today the seat of the General Civil War Archive — to be protected by two local policemen — as if the Catalans were about to forcefully make off with the papers!

It is also significant that it is not only the conservative Popular Party (PP) that has sought to legitimise the Francoist confiscation of Catalan documents. The Socialist party (PSOE) too is to some extent implicated, despite the fact that the Socialists themselves also suffered cruel repression and had their documents seized in Franco's military coup in 1936. It is sad proof of the fact that in the Spanish State, nationalistic and totalitarian ways have greater following than do ideological considerations such as solidarity, the need to reject brutal fascist ways or the definition of the concept of «archive unity» that is made, ignoring the rights of the archives originally plundered. Many officials in Madrid today, of whatever political hue, only seem to take into consideration arguments that the Francoist ideologists themselves would have been proud of coining. In addition, Madrid's position is also favoured by the corporative interests of the archivists of the National Archive, and, in particular, those of the archivists at Salamanca's Civil War archive.

Nevertheless, there have been exceptions to these attitudes in Spanish society, in sharp contrast to mainstream party politicians. First and foremost, there is Teresa Carvajal, a former independent city councillor for the PSOE on Salamanca city council. The first time the Dignity

Commission heard about the position of this praiseworthy defender of Castilian and Leonese heritage was in a letter that appeared in *La Vanguardia* a few days after the Dignity Commission's first press conference in Salamanca. In the letter headed «From Salamanca», Teresa Carvajal lodged a complaint about the official boycott of the Commission's visit to Salamanca on 14 October 2002. In her letter, the councillor asked: «How is it possible that local media failed to announce the dignified and democratic visit of a group of Catalans whose intention it was to inform the residents of Salamanca about why they want to recover part of their identity?». The letter concluded with an expression of thanks: «In the name of those of us who want this country's foundations to be based on dialogue and participation, we wish to show our gratitude for the heart-warming visit of this large group of people». The publication of this letter came as a breath of fresh air and was in stark contrast to the total boycott of the Commission's first press conference. The fact that a Salamanca city councillor, no less, had spoken out in favour of the Commission was seen as a sign that, officialdom aside, a warmer reception awaited the Catalan demands than had at first been thought.

Since then, the relationship between Teresa Carvajal and the Dignity Commission has become stronger, despite the fact that she had not been able to attend the press conference on 14 October 2002: no-one in her party, the Socialist PSOE, which had been officially invited, had informed her. At a later stage, she was the honorary hostess of the Commission's second visit to Salamanca, and took part in the protest against the opening of the «War Propaganda» exhibition on 12 November 2002. That evening, she organised the impromptu conference given by Carles Fontserè and Toni Strubell at Salamanca's legendary *Ateneo*. On the Commission's third visit, she gave an exhilarating speech in favour of dialogue and common sense. She again criticised the attitude of the local authorities and their «lack of courtesy» towards the Dignity Commission. Teresa Carvajal's co-operation and contributions have been constant and most positive ever since.

Another letter appeared in *La Vanguardia* on 26 October 2002. It came from another important source of support in Salamanca, that of José A. Frias, the director of the Library Science Department of the University of Salamanca, who was sympathetic to the Dignity Commission's position. In his letter, the professor pointed to the fact that in Salamanca there was more support for the return of the Catalan documents than one would think. «In many fields», the letter said, «there are professionals who have defended the return of the documents to Catalonia and we have made our position known in the past». He also expressed his concern at the fact that the decision to retain the Catalan documents in Salamanca had been taken without consulting his Department — Library and Document Science — and added that he considered the Salamanca documents to be «spoils of war» which should be «returned as soon as possible to their rightful owners».

The support given to the Commission's position by Salamanca journalist Aníbal Lozano was another outstanding feature of the campaign and the one which best illustrated the intolerance and aggressive nature of Salamanca's ruling class. In his *Tribuna de Salamanca* column, Aníbal Lozano on 13 October 2002 published an article that was favourable to the return of the Catalan documents: «What cannot be forgotten under any pretext is the Archive's origin and what it was used for, even in the postwar years: to nourish repression over the next forty years... It is like the moral heritage of what was taken from them, and, bearing this in mind, there should be no conditions attached to its transfer... Furthermore, it is unacceptable for Salamanca to retain confiscated original documents if it seeks to become a symbol of modern times.»

After publishing this article, Lozano was deprived of his daily column in the *Tribuna de Salamanca*. Barcelona's *La Vanguardia* newspaper partially redeemed the situation with an honourable offer to publish a weekly column of Lozano's, a gesture which Lozano accepted. One of his first columns was a passionate tribute to Carles Fontserè, the Catalan civil war artist associated with the Dignity Commission with whom he had recently had a meal and much of whose work is confiscated in Salamanca. Aníbal Lozano has since been in permanent contact with the Commission and has attended various meetings both in Salamanca and Barcelona.

Teresa Carvajal and Aníbal Lozano typify the very best of the Castilian tradition of a liberal spirit and a sense of brotherhood amongst nations, an attitude opposed to the imposition of Castile's «right of conquest» over the other national communities of the Iberian Peninsula. They represent a liberal tradition that exists in Castile which, though important, has tended to be overwhelmed by dictatorships and the militarist, austere and intolerant façade that history has favoured and made predominant in this country. Both of them struggle, each in their own way, for the democratization of Castile's mass media, and for the strengthening of the liberal tradition of Castile which, though demanding rights, heritage, history, and popular spirit, nevertheless rejects the bullying nature of her tyrants and its political embodiment in centralist thought. In an interview with Xavier Ayén, in *La Vanguardia* (18/10/2003), Aníbal Lozano expressed his objections to the political climate of Salamanca: «These documents of paper resulted in the torture and death of a lot of people, even of folk from Salamanca. It is a moral imperative that they return to their place of origin. Salamanca is showing itself to be an awfully conservative city, willing to defend something indefensible. There is fear. It is a society where many do not say what they think. I do. Why not? Are we not free to do so? The Salamanca right wing has nothing to do with Gallardón [liberal Madrid PP leader] or with the Catalan right wing. I wish it did! Here they want to preserve what Franco gave us when he turned us into a Fascist stronghold during the Civil War.»

To express its gratitude for their contributions, the Dignity Commission paid tribute to Teresa Carvajal and Aníbal Lozano at a memorable meeting in Barcelona's Ateneu on 22 May 2003. Before a full house, speeches were made by Toni Strubell and Jordi Porta, the President of Catalonia's largest cultural association, Òmnium Cultural. Members of different Catalan parties (CiU, ERC, ICV and mayor of Arbúcies, Jaume Soler) presented them with two plaques commemorating the event. The event received full-page coverage in *Avui* and *El Punt* newspapers.

Without leaving Salamanca, it is also most fitting to mention the position of one Salamanca-based party known as Izquierda Castellana (Castilian Left) and its support for the Dignity Commission. This party offered support to the Commission on its first trip to Salamanca on 14 October 2002. In addition, local officials of Izquierda Castellana courageously helped to carry the banner in protest at the opening of the «Propaganda en Guerra» exhibition on 12 November 2002. Izquierda Castellana also organised a meeting in favour of the return of the documents to Catalonia. With over three hundred people in the audience, the meeting included speeches by Catalan History Professor, Borja de Riquer, and Josep Maria Sans i Travé, Director of the Catalan National Archive. Professor José Luis de las Heras, Professor at Salamanca University's Geography and History Department, also participated in the meeting, showing slides labelled in Catalan. The response of the audience — mostly local students and intellectuals — was truly surprising both in terms of numbers and attitude. Applause for the three speakers' arguments was encouragingly warm. Dr. José Luis de las Heras has since been very active throughout the period 2002-2004 with articles in the press, participation in debates and radio programmes on the subject.

At a State level, Spanish support for the Dignity Commission's position was strengthened with a Manifesto signed in the summer of 2002 by over a hundred professors and university lecturers.[5] The Manifesto, published as a letter in Madrid's *El País*, demanded that the Spanish State should abide by the international treaties it had signed (The Hague International Agreement on the Protection of Cultural Goods in the event of Armed Conflict and UN General Assembly Resolution 4 6/10) and that the Spanish Government fulfil the agreement signed by the Spanish Cabinet on 15 March 1995 regarding the return to Catalonia of the Catalan archives held at Salamanca. This letter also called for the suspension of the exhibition *Propaganda en guerra* because «it had not received the authorisation (...) of the Catalan Government or the private individuals and legal entities affected by the Francoist confiscations in 1939».

Despite the fact that the Manifesto was signed by eminent academics such as Javier Tusell and Miguel Rodríguez y Herrero de Miñón, or politicians such as Gaspar Llamazares, it was only published in a few newspapers, thus limiting its repercussion. This confirmed a certain tendency in the Spanish media to play down a matter that was beginning to stir too many consciences and that was becoming increasingly hard to explain. In addition to their support for the Manifesto, Javier Tusell and Miguel Rodríguez y Herrero de Miñon also expressed their opinions on the question of the Salamanca Papers by signing the Dignity Commission's June Declaration, as well as writing articles and giving their opinions in interviews in the press and on television.

The demonstrations of 15 October 2002

One of the key moments in the Comission's campaign were the demonstrations on 15 October 2002. For the first time, the Dignity Commission had called a major demonstration to protest about the Government's failure to return Catalan documents from Salamanca. The day for the demonstration was not chosen at random. A number of factors made 15 October a suitable day, two of which stand out: it was the date

---

5. Although the campaign was conducted separately, the complete list is included in Appendix 2.

initially chosen for the opening of the «Propaganda en Guerra» exhibition as part of the Salamanca 2002 programme; and it was also the 62nd anniversary of the execution of Lluís Companys, President of Catalonia, a factor that seemed to add insult to injury. In co-operation with the Association Conèixer Catalunya (ACCAT), the Dignity Commission planned a day of protest in Barcelona. The aim was to make known to the Spanish government that the institutions and citizens of Catalonia objected to the Ministry of Culture's unilateral decision, announced through associated bodies, not to return any documents to Catalonia from the General Civil War Archive in Salamanca. Rallies were held at two different points: the first in front of the Government Delegation building, in Barcelona's Pla de Palau, at half past seven in the evening; the second gathering was held an hour later in Plaça del Rei, larger city spaces being unavailable at the time.

The Pla de Palau rally was a simple meeting at which a letter addressed to the President of the Spanish Government was read out. The letter expressed the Catalan people's indignation at the decision to retain their documents at Salamanca. The town councillor from Sallent — and Radio Sallent speaker — Salvador Arderiu, read the letter:

«To the Prime Minister of Spain:

Dear Sir,

The Dignity Commission is an organisation which arose from the heart of Catalan civil society and which, seeking to achieve the return of Catalan documentary heritage from the Republican period, has thought it fitting to send you this letter by way of the Office your Government has in the capital city of our nation. We wish to approach you and give our opinion on your Government's decision not to return the Catalan archives at present withheld in the newly created General Civil War Archive in Salamanca.

The people of Catalonia, their institutions and political and social organisations of every nature, feel profound regret and indignation at this decision. It cannot be forgotten, as is generally known, that these documents were seized by the army of occupation that entered Catalonia on the orders of rebel General Franco in 1938-1939. The archives of hundreds of city halls, those of practically all democratic political parties, those at the headquarters of unions, dozens of cultural associations with no involvement in politics, as well as the libraries and archives of private individuals and families of the most representative figures of Catalan nationalist, republican and democratic forces, were all ignominiously looted in an act of barbarism that was inspired by the Nazis themselves. Catalan political parties and society have never ceased to demand the return of these documents, and have unceasingly protested their confiscation as a means of exerting a wave of repression and physical elimination without precedent in our recent history. Use of these documents led to thousands of people being shot, interned in concentration camps or suffering repression of the most diverse forms in a never-ending series of criminal atrocities. Due to the way in which the political transition to democracy was conducted as from 1975, however, those responsible for these crimes have gone unpunished. We remind you of these events, Prime Minister, because the role that you have played has disappointed us, as indeed has the attitude of your government. Any government with a the least degree of humanity, sense of decency and justice would have immediately ordered the return of these documents to their rightful place. It should have done so if only out of respect for all those who gave their lives, and with a view to returning to their rightful place archives that were looted from and belong to a country that has always loved freedom and culture.

A few weeks ago, the Communication Officer of your party, Sr. Don Rafael Hernando, filled us all with hope when he made the following statement to the press: «Any possible step that may serve to console people still affected by situations arising from a conflict such as the civil war, to overcome their suffering or reconstruct their past and bring solace to their spirit, must be welcomed by and seen to by our Government.» But time has shown us that the hopes raised by these words were unfounded. If we are to judge by the respect that your government has shown for Catalan feeling, we must conclude that Catalans are not seen by your government as a «people». We have neither been well received nor well attended. No attention has been paid to our suffering nor to our need to «reconstruct our past», to use the words of Sr. Hernando. On the contrary. No one has brought solace to our spirit, as promised by Sr. Hernando, «solace» to overcome the trauma, human and material losses caused by the Civil War. Our sensitivity has not been in the least taken into consideration by the government you preside over. With this new case, your government — the greatest benefactor of the Francisco Franco Foundation, adorer of massive Spanish flags in Madrid's Plaza Colon and persecutor of those who have protested that the King was made to lie when he claimed, in an official speech, that the Spanish language had «never been imposed» nor the Catalan language persecuted — has decided to bless the «right of conquest» that has so characterised the Castilian way of understanding the Iberian peninsula and, alas, the world.

We want you to know, Prime Minister, that as regards the stolen Catalan archives, there are more reasons that fill many Catalans with indignation, and indeed, as has been seen recently, members of your own party. In Salamanca, a city one thousand kilometres from Barcelona, your government is promoting an exhibition called «Propaganda en guerra» («Propaganda in time of war»), which is about to be opened as part of the

Salamanca's 2002 European City of Culture programme. The reason for our indignation arises from the fact that, as you know portion, a significant of the materials involved form part of the archives stolen from the Catalan people by Franco. The fact that permission was not even solicited from the legitimate owners of these documents says little in favour of the sense of civility and respect of the organisers of this exhibition. This opinion is not only held by Catalans who are aware of the case. Many hundreds of European intellectuals and professors have condemned the dishonour involved in the fact that objects seized by Fascists are to be exhibited at a European City of Culture event. As has been asked by several high-ranking personalities from Greek public life, what would Melina Mércouri, creator of the European City of Culture event seventeen years ago, have thought of this? What would she say if she were alive? She strove to make this event a catalyst of brotherhood amongst nations that would promote the values of democracy and justice throughout Europe. What would she say today when the event is to be turned into a showcase for taunting and slighting our people and our democratic tradition?

As the indefatigable member of the Dignity Commission — artist Carles Fontserè — puts it, only an unworthy government would expose stolen posters and documents taken as loot. This wise observation should lead you, Prime Minister, to a profound reconsideration of your policy regarding this question, bearing in mind the basic criteria of UNESCO on the need to return to their rightful owners documents that have been stolen in time of conflict or war. The fact that the former Secretary General of that body Federico Mayor Zaragoza spoke out in favour of the return to Catalonia of the Catalan documents should have prompted you to react. But this has not been the case, and the world and history will have to judge your actions.

To finish this letter, Prime Minister, we wish to ask you a question that a large proportion of our people would like to see answered. What type of private property does your government respect? And what type of property is your government still likely to fail to respect? When will you admit that your argument in favour of one sole Civil War archive is unsound, when it is now public knowledge that your government is funding the Francisco Franco Archive to keep it private, and has better no intention to dissolve the five large Castilian archives that hold the best part of the documents on the Civil War? When will you be willing to admit that the appeal your government is making to an alleged spirit of «archive unity» is little more than a trick to justify a policy that has no justification?

Finally, we would also like to ask you when your party will be willing to condemn the Franco regime at the different parliaments that exist in Spain? And above all, when will you be willing to treat the Catalan nation, its language and legitimate heritage with the respect they deserve?

When you have answered these and other questions, maybe we will be able to counter some of the profound mistrust and attitudes of divorce that large numbers of the Catalan people feel towards your party's policies. At present, the most widely shared feelings arising from the question of the archives are those of incredulity and indignation.

Yours faithfully,

The Dignity Commission.

This letter was read out to thousands of people at the Pla de Palau. As it was being read, hundreds more continued to pour into the square from all directions. Among those present were politicians from all the Catalan parties — except PP, of course — and personalities from all walks of Catalan public life. When the letter had been read out, and enthusiastically applauded, it was delivered to the Spanish government's office in the square. The letter received no answer.

After that, the crowds in the Pla de Palau began to move towards Plaça del Rei, where at 8.30 p.m. there was to be a meeting with the slogan «Diguem no a la foscor del neofranquisme» («Let's say 'no' to the darkness of neo-Francoist Spain»). Observers say that the wide Via Laietana was blocked for half an hour as the demonstrators made their way there. Unfortunately, when those at the head of the column reached the avenue, they found that the streets on the other side were already jammed full. It had become impossible to reach the square, the only one that the city authorities had allowed to be used for such a meeting. This resulted in a situation where Plaça Sant Jaume, the square housing the Catalan government and Barcelona city hall, and all the adjacent streets, had to accommodate the large number of demonstrators who followed the meeting over loudspeakers. As *El Temps* magazine put it, people «could hardly believe what was happening: the Plaça del Rei was jam packed». According to *El Temps,* «the majority of demonstrators had to follow the meeting from adjacent streets, from windows and balconies, and from the Plaça Sant Jaume», where, with the aid of councillor Jordi Portabella, loudspeakers had been placed at the last minute to enable people to follow the meeting. This great response by the people of Barcelona and surrounding districts to the call was seen as a major success, all the more so considering the limited publicity that had been possible. Word of mouth, one advertisement in the newspaper *Avui* and e-mail had made the day possible.

The meeting «Diguem "no" a la foscor del neofranquisme» (Let's say 'no' to the darkness of neo-Francoist Spain) was called and organised by the Dignity Commission with the aid of ACCAT, a Catalan cultural organisation presided over by the venerable promoter of Catalan culture, Josep Espar Ticó. The meeting was presented by Joel Joan, a Catalan actor who stars in the most popular comedy series on Catalan TV, «Plats Bruts», that had recently won the prestigious Ondas Prize. He was the ideal man to strike the right balance between a sense of purpose and the informality required by a public meeting of this kind. For an occasion held under the traditional Catalan slogan of «Diguem no!» («Let's say no»), with singer Raimon and his song with that very title could not be missing. One of the high points of the evening was when it was sung, the audience signing the words at the top of its voice. Just then, thousands of sparklers were lit, an image that made the front pages of most of Barcelona's newspapers the next day. After that, three hundred members of the Catalan Choir Federation sang a choral version of the same song. The audience in the square and in all the adjacent streets chorused the song creating an electric atmosphere which was given intensive coverage by television and radio stations; one radio station, Catalunya Cultura, broadcast the whole meeting live. After two versions of «Diguem no!», one of the better known personalities to have been directly affected by the seizure of Catalan documents, Teresa Pàmies, winner of the prestigious Catalan Literature Prize, addressed the audience on behalf of the Dignity Commission. She read out the Manifesto «No a la foscor del neofranquisme» («Let's say 'no' to the darkness of neo-Francoist Spain») with great feeling and determination:

> Good evening, ladies and gentlemen. We are gathered here tonight at the summons of the Dignity Commission, in the historic Plaça del Rei, because there are things that cannot be accepted in the present situation of our country. We are gathered here because we could not continue to be silent spectators of a political situation which increasingly fills our hearts with anxiety and unrest. We are gathered here because we cannot tolerate injustice, because we are rebels against the impositions of a government that fails to respect our national dignity. The use made by the governing Partido Popular of the overall majority it won at the last elections has led to a situation which, we are obliged to denounce before our people, before the political authorities of the State and all Europe. We can no longer tolerate this dark shadow looming over us. The path towards democracy and the full recovery of national and social rights that many Catalans considered to be guaranteed by the 1978 constitution has turned out to be a path of growing uncertainty, darkness and increasingly undermined guarantees. If it is intolerable that the government party uses the constitution as a weapon against all those who do not think as it does, it must be seen as

even more hypocritical that leading members of this very party, particularly its current leader, were opposed to the constitution twenty-five years ago.

The past months have been marked by signs, gestures, laws and speeches that have filled us with foreboding and reservations. Nonetheless, no event has raised as much indignation as the government's refusal to return to Catalonia the documents and archives withheld at Salamanca. Some may feel this can be attributed to scientific criteria, but only a blind person could come to believe this. Professor Paul Preston has recently pointed out that there can be no reason for not returning the documents to Catalonia. This same historian headed the list of over 700 academics from across the world who, four months ago, backed a worldwide call denouncing the fact that the Spanish governent was unwilling to return archives which are the property of the Catalan people.

But in contrast to the dark prospect offered by the Aznar government, there are also numerous signs of hope as epitomised by, the massive turn-out for today's rallies in Barcelona. Moreover, we must also refer to a factor the Spanish government had clearly not been expecting: as time goes by, more and more people are beginning to lose their fear. More and more people are beginning to ask questions about their past and that of their country. Recent television broadcasts on the Catalan network have had massive audiences. People are beginning to talk about the mass graves which were the result of Franco's repression. Though they date from a time long before those of other regimes, such as those in Argentina, El Salvador or Chile, it has taken much longer for those in Spain to be known about. People are now beginning to ask why. If Pinochet's career can now be openly condemned, people are wondering why it is still taboo in Spain to condemn the dictatorship which preceded the present regime. People are beginning to grasp the great difficulties that the Catalan nation is exposed to in the present media, cultural and political framework under current legislation. (...)

The last person to speak at the meeting was Toni Strubell, co-ordinator of the Dignity Commission. He reflected on the meaning of the two historic protests — on 14 and 15 October 2002 — against the retention of Catalan archives in Salamanca and lamented the fact that in Salamanca the local authorities had not received the one hundred and sixty Catalans who had visited Salamanca the day before. Only the press had been present at the conference that was held in one of the city's major hotels, despite the fact that all the local authorities had been invited. He also gave thanks to the mayors and city councillors and other representatives of institutions, members of the Parliaments and Senate and, above all, to those directly affected by the confiscations, for having accompanied the Dignity Commission on the visit to Salamanca. He pointed out that the expedition to Salamanca had «surprised» people because it had been characterized by emotions and dignity. He referred to the speeches made there by Rosa Maria Carrasco, who had asked to see and recover the letter her father had addressed to her family shortly before dying before a firing squad in Burgos; or the words of Carles Fontserè calling for the return of the magnificent collection of his posters still withheld at Salamanca. Strubell also wished to show the Commission's gratitude to all the groups and individuals in Salamanca who had shown solidarity towards the Catalan demands, and also the 700 professors and intellectuals from around the world, headed by Mario Soares, Francesco Cossiga, Noam Chomsky, Nawal el Saadawi and Paul Preston, who had shown support for the Commission's Manifesto, and for whom Strubell called for a round of applause. In conclusion, he speculated on the possible future of the Catalan archives and mentioned the confusion over the issue in the Catalan section of the government party (PP), as shown in the recent contradictions between Ministers Piqué and Rajoy, who just before the beginning of the meeting had described the affair as «closed». Strubell spoke with irony of things that the PP may consider to be «closed», since in 1975 it would also appear that Franco's tomb had been «closed», despite the government's apparent temptations to open it and release the essence it contains. He ended his speech by saying that without the return of the Catalan documents from Salamanca, the confrontation that the Civil War represented could not be considered to be over, and that, therefore, the «right of conquest» still applied.

The meeting received massive coverage in the media. It was given front-page headlines in all the major Catalan newspapers, extensive reports in magazines, TV news and commentaries on radio chat shows, etc. The Dignity Commission and the ACCAT association were very grateful to Joel Joan, Raimon, Teresa Pàmies, the Catalan Choirs Federation and David Jou for their participation in this memorable event.

Further activities of the Dignity Commission

During the course of the years 2003 and 2004, the activities of the Dignity Commission have not ceased. It would be impossible to give details of all. On the one hand, the Commission participated in hundreds of meetings throughout the Catalan Countries.[6] Five meetings were also

---

6. An expression which includes, amonst other territories, Valencia, Majorca and the other Balearic Islands, the portion of Catalonia in France and Catalonia proper.

attended in Salamanca organised by local groups such as Ciudadanos por el Patrimonio, Izquierda Castellana and Foro de Izquierdas-Los Verdes. Some of these events took place in the magnificent setting of buildings as emblematic as the Salamanca Atheneum Club — where Carles Fontserè made a memorable speech — or the Faculty of Geography and History of Salamanca University. One debate with archivists and university professors, held on 17 June 2004, was broadcast on Salamanca's local TV station. As regards other meetings, two warm tributes staged in Barcelona stand out. The first was paid to journalist Aníbal Lozano and city councillor Teresa Carvajal, both of Salamanca, and was held in the Barcelona Atheneum Club on 22 May 2003. The second tribute was paid to Southampton University Emeritus Professor Henry Ettinghausen, and was held at the Farinera del Clot in Barcelona on 19 December 2003. Both tributes were very well attended and speeches were delivered by Toni Strubell, professor Til Stegmann, of Frankfurt University, Matthew Tree — the prize-winning English author who writes in Catalan — and Henry Ettinghausen himself. Xavier Borràs read a poem dedicated to Ettinghausen which had been written by Montserrat Milian. These tributes had been designed to show gratitude for these people's support for the Dignity Commission.

The official campaign for the return of the documents also continued its course. Many institutions and bodies, following the Dignity Commission's recommendations, took the first steps to enable legal proceedings to start with official demands for the return of their property. Amongst those involved were the political parties ERC and PSUC, trade unions UGT and CADCI, city halls such as Tarragona — amongst others — as well as private individuals such as the Capo and Cambó families. A report was also sent to the president of the Council of Europe's Culture department, Ms Viviane Reding, calling for Europe's involvement in this issue. Apart from this, the meeting held on 13 April 2004 with Nobel Prize-winner Adolfo Pérez Esquivel must also be mentioned. Mr Pérez informed the Commission[7] of his intention to write a public letter to the Spanish president, Mr José Luis Rodríguez Zapatero, reminding him of his duty as president to have the documents returned to the Catalan

---

7. Accompanied by representatives of the Catalan parties supporting the Commission: Dolors Comas and Josep Altayó (ICV), Josep Camps (CIU), Xavier Menéndez (PSC) and Elisenda Romeu (ERC).

people. The letter was duly sent and widely referred to in the Catalan and Spanish press the following week.

As regards political contacts, several meetings held at the highest level stand out. The first was called in Madrid by Culture Minister Carmen Calvo on 26 May 2004. This meeting was to last over two hours. In representation of the Commission, two former presidents of the Catalan Parliament, Heribert Barrera and Joan Rigol, and the current vice-President of the Valencian Parliament, Mr Joaquim Puig, were present, as were the president of the Catalan Archivists' Association, Joan Boadas, Salamanca University history professor, Dr. José Luis de las Heras, Jordi Font, director of the Theatre Institute, and five members of the Commission's Secretariat. On 28 June 2004, the Dignity Commission also held a meeting with Catalan Culture Minister, Ms Caterina Mieras, at the Ministry in Barcelona's Rambles. Both these meetings were designed to prepare the way for the creation of a negotiation committee to decide on the question of the return of the «Salamanca Papers» to Catalonia and Valencia.

FUTURE PROSPECTS

This book appears in the autumn of 2004 at a crucial moment in the call for the return of the Catalan documents held in Salamanca. Soon decisions regarding them are soon to be announced by the Spanish Government.[1] It is to be hoped that they will not entail a solution that merely involves political bartering «to make all the parties happy» — as has been suggested — nor a symbolic arrangement based on compromise. The Dignity Commission wishes to underline once more that we do not consider ourselves to be before a banal case requiring the crutch of artificial «balance». The Dignity Commission wishes to reiterate its view that the case it has espoused is no banal one that requires the crutch of artificial «balance». It is rather a case that has transcendent ethical and political implications. If the result is not fully satisfactory, it will be regarded with profound disappointment by those sectors that have been awaiting a solution for sixty-five years. National dignity, historical truth and justice are in jeopardy and whatever decisions are made now will surely affect the climate of political coexistence between Catalans and Spaniards in the future. Now is also a moment in which to evaluate the prospects of the Dignity Commission, an organisation which so many groups and people helped to create in January 2002.

The Dignity Commission has always considered that there is little to discuss regarding the place where the documents in question should be housed in future. If one day they left our country on a journey that should never have been made, it is surely to our country that they must all return today. If one day they were taken from our country on a journey that should never have been made, it is surely to our country that they must

---

1. There has been talk in Government circles of the need to find a «final solution» to this question since the March 14th victory of the Socialists at the General Elections.

one day return. This may appear to be a maximalist position to those who regard this question in terms of a classical negotiation based on consensus in which a few sensible gestures would be enough to restore peace. For the Dignity Commission, and for the hundreds of organisations and institutions it represents in Catalonia and Valencia, this is the only acceptable solution in an age when Germany has apologised to the Basques for Gernika, the Vatican to the Jews for the Inquisition and Tony Blair to the Irish for the Great Famine. Although some sources have spoken of the need to return to the Catalans those «more symbolic» documents such as the original of Catalonia's 1932 Statute of Autonomy or the «Generalitat Government papers» — a reference to the (in)famous 507 batches of documents that are often mentioned as if they accounted for all the Catalan documents held in Salamanca —[2] the Dignity Commission is convinced that the Catalan people demand the return of all the stolen documents. How can one differentiate legally between returnable stolen goods and non-returnable stolen goods? To put it in more explicit terms — as professor Josep Maria Terricabras has done on more than one occasion — the case of the Salamanca documents must be defined as if one was dealing with the case of a pick-pocketed wallet: neither the time that has passed since it was stolen nor the use to which it is now being put can justify its ongoing retention. In a law-abiding state, stolen goods are returned to their owners in full. The fact that today that wallet may happen to be on show in a museum or stowed in an archive in no way changes matters. All too often, however, we hear it said that the wallet cannot be returned because it performs a scientific and social «service».

In answer to this, and as regards the question of these services, the Dignity Commission is convinced that once the documents are repatriated, they will continue to be offered most competently by our own national institutions, particularly the National Archive at Sant Cugat. Our historical heritage cannot be better served than by the return of the documents. Withholding them in Salamanca has contributed nothing to furthering research into our history. On the contrary, as intended by those who pillaged them, it has contributed to concealing it and to enhancing the attempts to eliminate our national identity through cultural genocide. The return of the documents will not entail any loss of efficiency, as is sometimes alleged, and historical justice justice before history? will also be served.

---

2. When it is a known fact that they only account for a small part of the documents and possibly not the most valuable ones.

If the Spanish Government's imminent decision does not ensure the return of all the documents, the Dignity Commission will continue to call for their repatriation using all the legal means in its power. We believe that openly stating this intention is the most honourable way of expressing our determination to exercise a democratic right. We have explained our position to members of the Spanish and Catalan Governments at the highest level during meetings held in the months of May and June 2004 respectively. No one should, therefore, denounce our action as disloyal or unexpected if we are obliged to take legal proceedings.

The Dignity Commission has for almost three years been highlighting the need to exercise the rights of individuals and institutions affected by the confiscations. Legal experts of differing ideological persuasions have encouraged us in this direction whenever we have sought their advice. We have at all times been assured that we have a «very clear» legal case for devolution. Attempts to make us believe that our claim is disqualified by the fact that the Spanish «Democratic Transition» assumed aspects of Francoist legality that had not been rooted out in new democratic laws — as is suggested in some circles — not only fail to make any sense, but can only be seen as morally offensive, as are all attempts to whitewash the Francoist regime's criminal record. It is in this light that we must judge the claims for the recovery of their archives made by parties and unions such as CNT, ERC, Esquerra Valenciana, PSUC, UGT or CADCI,[3] or private individuals such as the heirs of the Cambó, Rovira or Capo families, all of which, along with many others, are assessed today are now being assessed? by the Dignity Commission. We believe that the Spanish Government would be mistaken to opt for an unjust solution that would give rise to negative international reaction. This would be the case if parties affected by Fascist pillaging were left no other option than to resort to the international law courts to retrieve their looted documents sixty-five years later.

A key step for the Dignity Commission in the near future will be the mailing out of this book to all those who supported us by signing our Manifesto in the summer of 2002. Among our supporters are ex-presidents Mário Soares and Francesco Cossiga and Nobel prize-winners Adolfo Pérez Esquivel and Rigoberta Menchú, as well as hundreds of university professors from over 220 universities worldwide. If you signed

---

3. All of which are legal organisations today.

our Manifesto, we wish to express our deepest gratitude to you. We would like you to know that our Manifesto has made a deep impression on Spanish public opinion. In October 2002, an American journalist commented that the struggle of the Dignity Commission to effect the return of the archives was «the initiative that has done most to situate the Catalan cause on the map in the last twenty-five years». Your support has been vital in bringing this about.

We cannot conclude this epilogue without mentioning some of the more positive repercussions that have resulted from the Dignity Commission's struggle. It has been a lesson and an honour for us to receive so much support in this campaign: national institutions — the Catalan Parliament and Government — city and town halls, private victims of the pillaging, unions and parties — affected or not — historians of every speciality, archivists and academics from all over the world and thousands of groups and individuals throughout the country have shown us their warmest support. We hope to be able to continue to enjoy this support if further efforts are still needed to recover our historical identity. It has also been a privilege to have the chance to come into contact with groups and individuals in Salamanca who also struggle for dignity and to strengthen democracy in their home and who have sometimes suffered for so doing, as in Aníbal Lozano's case. These men and women have joined ranks with us on the road to the recovery of fuller collective and individual freedom and historical memory. We take pride in the fact that the question of the «Salamanca Papers» has allowed issues to be raised in Salamanca itself, there having been a positive outcome in some sectors of public opinion and the mass media after a rather shaky start in 2002.

We do not know what the future holds for the Dignity Commission as of 2005. If further struggle is necessary for the return of all Catalan documents from Salamanca, we shall continue to regard it as a further step in the recovery of our national dignity.

Secretariat of the Dignity Commission:

Toni Strubell (co-ordinator), Imma Albó, Anna Almazan, Josep Altayó, Salvador Arderiu, Agustí Barrera, Enric Borràs, Xavier Borràs, Josep Camps, Josep Cruanyes, Ramon Escudé, Francesc Ferrer, Joaquim Ferrer, Julià Garcia, Josep Guia, Francesc Guilera, Antoni Martínez, Paula Martínez Ros, Abel Maruny, Xavier Menéndez, Montserrat Milian, Rosa Maria Puig-Serra, Marta Rojals, Claudi Romeu, Elisenda Romeu, Lluís Serra.

Barcelona-Valencia, September 2004

APPENDIX 1

LIST OF INTERNATIONAL PERSONALITIES WHO SUPPORT THE DIGNITY COMMISSION'S MANIFESTO FOR THE RETURN OF THE «SALAMANCA PAPERS» (JUNE 2002)

Hebe de Bonafini, President, Madres de la Plaza de Mayo

DAVID CARDÚS, Emeritus Professor, Baylor College, Texas

NOAM CHOMSKY, Professor, Massachusetts Institute of Technology

FRANCESCO COSSIGA, Emeritus President of the Italian Republic

FRANÇOISE DAVID, President, Quebecois Federation of Women

PETER GABRIEL, Musician

Baroness GLORIA HOOPER, Former EU Commissioner

FEDERICO MAYOR ZARAGOZA, Former Secretary General of UNESCO

RIGOBERTA MENCHÚ, Winner of the Nobel Prize for Peace, 1992

DANIELLE MITTERAND, President of France Libertés

GEORGES MOUSTAKI, Musician

JOAN ORÓ, Emeritus Professor, University of Houston

SGOURIDIS PANAGIOTY, Former Vice-President of the Greek Parliament

ADOLFO PÉREZ ESQUIVEL, Winner of the Nobel Prize for Peace, 1981

JAMES PETRAS, Professor, Binghampton University

PAUL PRESTON, Professor, London School of Economics

JOAN RIGOL, President of the Catalan Parliament

NAWAL EL SAAWADI, Writer, Human Rights activist

MARIO SOARES, Former President of Portugal

MIKIS THEODORAKIS, Musician

VIRGINIA TSOUDEROS, Former Foreign Vice-Minister, Greece

HOWARD ZINN, Emeritus Professor, University of Boston

INTERNATIONAL ACADEMIC COMMUNITY GIVING SUPPORT TO THE DIGNITY COMMISSION'S MANIFESTO FOR THE RETURN OF THE "SALAMANCA PAPERS"

Professor Mikel Aizpuru, Euskal Herriko Unibertsitatea (Basque Country)

Professor Giuliana Albini, Università degli Studi di Milano (Italy)

Professor Jane Albrecht, Wake Forest University (USA)

Professor Alain Alcouffe, Pôle Universitaire Européen (France)

Professor Anastasio Alemán, Universidad Autónoma, Madrid (Spanish State)

Professor Jens Allwood, Goeteborg University (Sweden)

Professor Rosario Alonso Ibáñez, Universidad de Oviedo (Spanish State)

Professor Juanjo Álvarez, Euskal Herriko Unibertsitatea (Basque Country)

Professor José Álvarez Junco, Universidad Complutense, Madrid (Spanish State)

Professor Josu Amezaga, Euskal Herriko Unibertsitatea (Basque Country)

Professor Bruno Anatra, Università di Cagliari (Italy)

Professor Fernando Andrés Robres, Universidad Autónoma, Madrid (Spanish State)

Professor Edward Andrew, Toronto University (Canada)

Professor Manuel Ariza Viguera, Universidad de Sevilla (Spanish State)

Professor Mikel Arriaga Landeta, Euskal Herriko Unibertsitatea (Basque Country)

Professor Carmen Arteaga Quintana, EU de Magisterio de Toledo (Spanish State)

Professor Irena Backus, Université de Genève (Switzerland)

Professor Sebastian Balfour, London School of Economics (England)

Professor Luis Bandrés Unanue, Euskal Herriko Unibertsitatea (Basque Country)

Professor Hassan Banhakeia, Université Mohamed I, Oujda (Morocco)

Professor Marco Bassi, Università di Bologna (Italy)

Professor Román Basurto, Euskal Herriko Unibertsitatea (Basque Country)

Professor Ole J. Benedictow, University of Oslo (Norway)

Professor Aitor Bengoetxea, Euskal Herriko Unibertsitatea (Basque Country)

Professor Cecilia Benoit, University of Victoria (Canada)

Professor Maryellen Bieder, Indiana University (USA)

Professor Paul W. Birt, University of Ottawa (Canada)

Professor Thomas N. Bisson, Harvard University (USA)

Professor David Blackbourn, Harvard University (USA)

Professor James Borchert, Cleveland State University (USA)

Professor Paula Botteri, Università degli Studi di Trieste (Italy)

Professor Enric Bou, Brown University (USA)

Professor Abdellah Bounfour, INALCO de Paris (France)

Professor Denise Boyer, Université d'Orléans (France)

Professor David Brookshaw, University of Bristol (England)

Professor J. G. M. de Bruijn, Free University of Amsterdam (Holland)

Professor Blas Cabrera Montoya, Universidad de La Laguna (Spanish State)

Professor Gregorio Cámara Villar, Universidad de Granada (Spanish State)

Professor Xuan Carlos Busto Cortina, Universidad de Oviedo (Spanish State)

Professor Paul Cammack, University of Manchester (England)

Professor José Miguel Campillo Robles, Mondragon Unibertsitatea (Basque Country)

Professor Arantza Campos, Euskal Herriko Unibertsitatea (Basque Country)

Professor Nicholas Canny, National University of Ireland, Galway (Eire)

Professor Diego Iván Cantabrana Armas, Universidad de La Rioja (Spanish State)

Professor David Cardús, Baylor College of Medicine, Texas (USA)

Professor Richard A. Cardwell, University of Nottingham (England)

Professor Fidel Castro Rodríguez, Universidad de Vigo (Galicia)

Professor Antonio Cazorla-Sánchez, Universidad de Granada (Spanish State)

Professor Salem Chaker, Institut National INALCO, Paris (France)

Professor Francisco Checa Olmos, Universidad de Almería (Spanish State)

Professor Noam A. Chomsky, Massachusetts Institute of Technology (USA)

Professor Evangelos Chrysos, Institute for Byzantine Studies, Athens (Greece)

Professor David Close, Memorial University of Newfoundland (Canada)

Professor Carlos Coello Martín, Universidad de la Rioja (Spanish State)

Professor Anna Cornagliotti, Università di Torino (Italy)

Professor Chris Corrin, University of Glasgow (Scotland)

Professor Ramon Cotarelo, Universidad Complutense, Madrid (Spanish State)

Professor Rosa Cristóbal Fuertes, Deustuko Unibertsitatea (Basque Country)

Professor Victoria Degrazia, Columbia University, New York (USA)

Professor Dimitris Dialetis, Kapodistrian University of Athens (Greece)

Professor John Dickinson, Université de Montréal (Quebec)

Professor Henk · van Dijk, Erasmus University, Amsterdam (Holland)

Professor Paul J. Dubé, University of Alberta (Canada)

Professor Michel Duquette, Université de Montréal (Quebec)

Professor Manuel Duran, Yale University (USA)

Professor Jose d'Encarnaçao, Universidade de Coimbra (Portugal)

Professor Stathis Efstathiadis, Aristotle University of Thessaloniki (Greece)

Professor Jens Engberg, University of Aarhus (Denmark)

Professor Xosé Estévez, Deustuko Unibertsitatea (Basque Country)

Professor Bradley Scott Epps, Harvard Univerity (USA)

Professor Piet Erasmus, University of the Free State (South Africa)

Professor Henry Ettinghausen, Southampton University (England)

Professor Richard Falk, Princeton University (USA)

Professor Robert Felkel, Michigan State University (USA)

Professor Pat Hudson, Cardiff University (Wales)

Professor Margaret R. Hunt, Amherst College (USA)

Professor José Idoyaga Arrospide, Euskal Herriko Unibertsitatea (Basque Country)

Professor Jaime Jaramillo Uribe, Universidad de los Andes (Columbia)

Professor Claude Javeau, Université Libre de Bruxelles (Belgium)

Professor Alf Johansson, Oslo University (Norway)

Professor Fred Judson, University of Alberta (Canada)

Professor Jyrki Käkönen, J. Monnet Centre, University of Tampere (Finland)

Professor Tom Keating, University of Alberta (Canada)

Professor Hans Keman, Universiteit Amsterdam (Holland)

Professor Liam Kennedy, Queen's University, Belfast (Eire)

Professor J. M. Klinkenberg, Université de Liège (Belgium)

Professor Edorta Kortadi Olano, Deustuko Unibertsitatea (Basque Country)

Professor J. Victor Koschmann, Cornell University (USA)

Professor Georg Kremnitz, Universitaet Wien (Àustria)

Professor Dominick LaCapra, Cornell University (USA)

Professor Reyes Lázaro Gurtubay, Smith College, Massachusetts (USA)

Professor Juan Lechago, Baylor College, Houston (USA)

Professor Paco Letamendia, Euskal Herriko Unibertsitatea (Basque Country)

Professor Chee Seng Lim, University of Malaya (Malaya)

Professor María Teresa López Soto, Universidad de Sevilla (Spanish State)

Professor Emilio Majuelo Gil, Nafarroko Unibertsitate Publikoa (Spanish State)

Professor Shirley Mangini, California State University (USA)

Professor Tahar Mansouri, Université de la Mannouba, Tunis (Tunísia)

Professor L. Marcheselli Loukas, Università di Trieste (Italy)

Professor Javier Márquez Quevedo, Universidad de Las Palmas (Spanish State) Universidad de Las Palmas (Spanish State)

Professor Elisa Martí López, Chicago University (USA)

Professor María Antonia Martínez Núñez, Universidad de Málaga (Spanish State)

Professor G. Matteo Allone, Università di Messina (Italy)

Professor F. Mazzanti Pepe, Università degli Studi di Genova (Italy)

Professor Markku Mattila, University of Tampere (Finland)

Professor Anthony McFarlane, University of Warwick, Coventry (England)

Professor David McNally, York University, Toronto (Canada)

Professor Kathleen McNerney, University of West Virginia (USA)

Professor and Vice-Dean Ludger Mees, Euskal Herriko Unibertsitatea (Basque Country)

Professor V. Fernando Migura Zanguitu, Euskal Herriko Unibertsitatea (Basque Country)

Professor Jane Millar, University of Bath (England)

Professor Kerby A. Miller, University of Missouri (USA)

Professor Abdallah el Mountassir, Université Ibnou Zohṛ, Agadir (Morocco)

Professor Patricia Moynagh, Bucknell University (USA)

Professor C. Moreiras Menor, Yale University (USA)

Professor Juan Carlos Monedero, Universidad Complutense, Madrid (Spanish State)

Professor José Miguel Morales Folguera, Universidad de Málaga (Spanish State)

Professor Philip Morgan, Westmintser College (USA)

Professor Tom Moring, University of Helsinki (Finland)

Professor Ulises Moulines, Universität Munchen (Germany)

Professor Daniel Mulholland, Tufts University (USA)

Professor Josep Maria Murià, Director Colegio de Jalisco, Guadalajara (Mexico)

Professor Angel Nepomuceno, Universidad de Sevilla (Spanish State)

Professor Geraldine Nichols, University of Florida (USA)

Professor Giancarlo Nonnoi, Università di Cagliari (Italy)

Professor Liisa L. North, York University, Toronto (Canada)

Professor Paul E. O'Donnell, University of Michigan, Flint (USA)

Professor David Olster, University of Kentucky (USA)

Professor Edmond Orban, Université de Montréal (Quebec)

Professor José Luis Orella Unzue, Deustuko Unibertsitatea (Basque Country)

Professor Eduardo Orellana Fernández, Universidad de Almería (Spanish State)

Professor Manuel Ortiz Heras, Universidad de Castilla-La Mancha (Spanish State)

Professor J. Osmond, Cardiff University (Wales)

Professor William Outhwaite, University of Sussex (England)

Professor Neil Parsons, University of Botswana (Botswana)

Professor Jaime Pastor Verdú, UNED (Spanish State)

Professor Stanley G. Payne, University of Wisconsin, Madison (USA)

Professor John Peeler, Bucknell University (USA)

Professor William Pencak, Penn State University (USA)

Professor James Petras, Binghampton University (USA)

Professor Carme Pi Sunyer, Chicago University (USA)

Professor Jaroslaw Piekalkiewicz, University of Kansas (USA)

Professor Claudine Potvin, University of Alberta (Canada)

Professor Paul Preston, London School of Economics (England)

Professor Maurizio Punzo, Università degli Studi di Milano (Italy)

Professor Martina Renouprez, Universidad de Cádiz (Spanish State)

Professor Joan Ramon Resina, Cornell University (USA)

Professor Margaret Reynolds, University of Queensland (Australia)

Professor Alícia Rodríguez, Universidad Gran Canarias (Spanish State)

Professor Drago Roksandic, University of Zagreb (Croatia)

Professor Francisco Rubio Cuenca, Universidad de Cádiz (Spanish State)

Professor Rafael Sainz de Rozas, Euskal Heriko Unibertsitatea (Basque Country)

Professor Xavier Sala Martin, Columbia University, New York (USA)

Professor Patxi Salaberri, Nafarrok Unibertsitate Publikoa (Spanish State)

Professor Ignacio Salazar, Universidad de Sevilla (Spanish State)

Professor O. Saldarriaga Vélez, Universidad Javeriana de Bogotá (Columbia)

Professor Immaculada Sánchez Alarcón, Universidad de Málaga (Spanish State)

95

Professor Isidro Sánchez Sánchez, Universidad de Castilla-La Mancha (Spanish State)

Professor Mario Santana, University of Chicago (USA)

Professor Giulio Sapelli, Università degli Studi di Milano (Italy)

Professor Luis Sarriés, Universidad de Navarra (Spanish State)

Professor Ralph Sarkonak, University of British Columbia (Canada)

Professor Nelia Saxby, Cape Town University (South Africa)

Professor Maya Shah, Maharaja Sayajirao University, Baroda (Índia)

Professor J. M. Sobrer, Indiana University (USA)

Professor Hartmut Soell, Heidelberg Universität (Germany)

Professor J. Sola Casadevall, Pennsylvania State University (USA)

Professor Howard M. Solomon, Tufts University (USA)

Professor Sergio Solbes Ferri, Universidad Gran Canarias (Spanish State)

Professor V. H. Sonawane, Maharaja Sayajirao University, Baroda (Índia)

Professor Christine Stansell, Princeton University (USA)

Professor Peter Stansky, Stanford University (USA)

Professor Tilbert D. Stegmann, J. W. Goethe Universität, Frankfurt (Germany)

Professor Barry H. Steiner, California State University (USA)

Professor Hillel Steiner, University of Manchester (England)

Professor Gerhard Steingress, Universidad de Sevilla (Spanish State)

Professor Gerry Stoker, University of Manchester (England)

Professor Benjamin Stora, Institut INALCO, Paris (France)

Professor R. Sugranyes de Franch, Fribourg Universität (Switzerland)

Professor Carlos Taibo Arias, Universidad Autónoma, Madrid (Spanish State)

Professor Janet Tallman, John F. Kennedy University (USA)

Professor Benjamín Tejerina, Euskal Herriko Unibertsitatea (Basque Country)

Professor Maria del Mar Torreblanca López, Universidad de Sevilla (Spanish State)

Professor Javier Tusell, Universidad Autónoma, Madrid (Spanish State)

Professor Michael Ugarte, University of Missouri (USA)

Professor Mario Vassallo, University of Malta (Malta)

Professor M. Vidal-Tibbits, Howard University (USA)

Professor Xulio Viejo Fernández, Universidad de Oviedo (Spanish State)

Professor Salvador Vinardell Crespo, Universidad de Salamanca (Spanish State)

Professor John K. Walton, University of Central Lancashire (England)

Professor Dana Ward, ISPP, Pitzer College (USA)

Professor William B. Watson, Massachusetts Institute of Technology (USA)

Professor Robert H. Whealey, Ohio University (USA)

Professor M. G. Whisson, Rhodes University (South Africa)

Professor Arthur Williamson, California State University, Sacramento (USA)

Professor Rodney Williamson, University of Ottawa (Canada)

Professor Peter Winn, Tufts University (USA)

Professor Alan Yates, University of Sheffield (England)

Professor Iñaki Zabaleta Urquiola, Euskal Herriko Unibertsitatea (Basque Country)

Professor Maria Begoña Zalbadea, Euskal Herriko Unibertsitatea (Basque Country)

Professor Claudio Zaccaria, Università degli Studi di Trieste (Italy)

Professor Raina Zimmering, Humboldt Universität, Berlín (Germany)

Professor Howard Zinn, Boston Universitat (USA)

Professor Moshe Zuckermann, University of Tel Aviv (Israel)

Associate Professor Korwa G. Adar, Rhodes University (South Africa)

Associate Professor W. Anselmi, University of Alberta (Canada)

Associate Professor Eric A. Arnold, Denver University (USA)

Associate Professor D. Baillargeon, Université de Montréal (Quebec)

Associate Professor S. Bielen, Warsaw University (Poland)

Associate Professor Guiomar Fages, University of Richmond (USA)

Associate Professor S. G. Feldman, University of Virginia (USA)

Associate Professor J. Carlos Fernández Serrato, Universidad de Sevilla (Spanish State)

Associate Professor L. Ferrari, Università di Trieste (Italy)

Associate Professor J. Gabilondo, University of Nevada (USA)

Associate Professor G. Garavaglia, Università degli Studi Milano (Italy)

Associate Professor Brian Gill, French University of Calgary (Canada)

Associate Professor J. A. Gutiérrez, University of Texas (USA)

Associate Professor Lázaro Lagóstena Barrios, Universidad de Cádiz (Spanish State)

Associate Professor Larry Hannant, University of Victoria (Canada)

Associate Professor Mark F. Jenkins, University of Washington, Seattle (USA)

Associate Professor Gail Kellough, York University, Toronto (Canada)

Associate Professor Kathi Kern, Kentucky University (USA)

Associate Professor Miran Komac, University of Ljubljana (Slovenia)

Associate Professor Tina Krontiris, Aristotle University, Theassaloniki (Greece)

Associate Professor Altieri Leonardo, Università di Bologna (Italy)

Associate Professor Mark Leier, Simon Fraser University (Canada)

Associate Professor Gary P. Leupp, University of Michigan (USA)

Associate Professor D. Londei, Università di Bologna (Italy)

Associate Professor R. Maddox, Carnegie Mellon University (USA)

Associate Professor Pedro Martínez Ruano, Universidad de Almería (Spanish State)

Associate Professor M. M-Tsilipakou, Aristotle University of Thessaloniki (Greece)

Associate Professor Marina Milan, Università degli Studi di Genova (Italy)

Associate Professor Kay McCormick, University of Cape Town (South Africa)

Associate Professor N. Moacanin, Zagreb University (Croatia)

Associate Professor Dorthy Noyes, Ohio State University (USA)

Associate Professor Gorka Orueta Estibariz, Euskal Herriko Unibertsitatea (Basque Country)

Associate Professor Robin Palmer, Rhodes University (South Africa)

Associate Professor D. Pastourmatzi, Aristotle University, Thessaloniki (Greece)

Associate Professor Miguel Peyró García, Universidad de Sevilla (Spanish State)

Associate Professor V. Petrousenko, Plovdiv University (Bulgaria)

Associate Professor M. S. Piretti, Università degli Studi de Bologna (Italy)

Associate Professor H. I. Radatz, Katholische Universität Eichstätt (Germany)

Associate Professor Raanan Rein

Associate Professor Jean-Claude Rixte, Tel Aviv University (Israel)

Université d'Avignon (France)

Associate Professor Edwin Roberts, California State University (USA)

Associate Professor E. Rodríguez, Cornell University (USA)

Associate Professor Daniel Rowland, University of Kentucky (USA)

Associate Professor Joana Sabadell, University of Albany (USA)

Associate Professor Mario Santana, University of Chicago (USA)

Associate Professor Lidia Santos, Yale University (USA)

Associate Professor Cristina Sanz, Georgetown University (USA)

Associate Professor Samir Saul, Université de Montréal (Quebec)

Associate Professor E. Steinhart, Texas Technical University (USA)

Associate Professor Nadia Urbinati, Columbia University, New York (USA)

Associate Professor J. C. Visser, Eramus Universiteit, Rotterdam (Holland)

Associate Professor P. Wahl Willis, University of Calgary (Canada)

Associate Professor Charles Zika, University of Melbourne (Australia)

Assistant Professor Angela Bagues, University of Pennsylvania (USA)

Assistant Professor L. Bayard de Volo, University of Kansas (USA)

Assistant Professor I. van Biezen, University of Birmingham (England)

Assistant Professor Gregory Blue

Assistant Professor Verity Burgmann

Assistant Professor Eduardo Canel, University of Victoria (Canada)

Melbourne University (Australia)

York University, Toronto (Canada)

Assistant Professor A. Cazorla-Sánchez, York University, Toronto (Canada)

Assistant Professor Raymond Craib, Cornell University (USA)

Assistant Professor Susan DiGiacomo, Amherst College (USA)

Assistant Professor Eleanor Dickey, Columbia University, New York (USA)

Assistant Professor Jonathan Earle, University of Kansas (USA)

Assistant Professor Marcia Epstein, Calgary University (Canada)

Assistant Professor Sebastian Faber, Oberlin College (USA)

Assistant Professor Ben Fallaw, Colby College (USA)

Assistant Professor Roger Friedlein, Freie Universität, Berlin (Germany)

Assistant Professor B. Fuerst-Bjelis, University of Zagreb (Croatia)

Assistant Professor S. Gingerich, University of Kansas (USA)

Assistant Professor Karen Graubart, Cornell University (USA)

Assistant Professor T. Harrington, Trinity College, Hartford (USA)

Assistant Professor David Hay, University of Lethbridge, Alberta (Canada)

Assistant Professor Gina Herrmann, University of Oregon (USA)

Assistant Professor Dick Houtman, Erasmus University, Rotterdam (Holland)

Assistant Professor James P. Huzel, University of British Columbia (Canada)

Assistant Professor Guillermo Irizarry, Yale University (USA)

Assistant Professor P. Kumaraswami, University of Wolverhampton (England)

Assistant Professor Élisabeth Le, University of Alberta (Canada)

Assistant Professor A. Maiello, Università di Genova (Italy)

Assistant Professor Stephen Miller, University of Maine (USA)

Assistant Professor Oktay Özel, Bilkent University, Ankara (Turkey)

Assistant Professor Darryl Reed, York University, Toronto (Canada)

Assistant Professor Cacilda Rego, University of Kansas (USA)

Assistant Professor Baki Tezcan, University of Wisconsin, Milwaukee (USA)

Assistant Professor Thang Vu, Vietnam National University, Hanoi (Vietnam)

Assistant Professor D. G. Wetherell, University of Calgary (Canada)

Dr. Paul Addison, Director, WW2 Studies, Edinburgh University (Scotland)

J. M. Albert, Economist, Atlanta (USA)

Cristina Amondarain, Tutor, Edinburgh University (Scotland)

Maritza Arrigunaga, Researcher, University of Texas Special Collections (USA)

Dr. A. Astvaldsson, Lecturer, University of Liverpool (England)

Dr. D. Atkinson, Senior Lecturer, University of Limerick (Eire)

E. Avila López, Researcher, University of Durham (England)

M. Aymamí, ESC, Grenoble (France)

M. A. Babi Vila, Tutor, Swansea University (Wales)

Dr. Susan Bannatyne, Fellow, University of Aberdeen (Scotland)

Professor Carmelo Barbera, Forli (Italy)

Dr. Richard Baxell, Researcher, London School of Economics (England)

Patricia Bennis, Archivist, University of Limerick (Eire)

Maura de Bernart, Researcher, Università di Bologna (Italy)

P. S. Bernard, Lecturer, Rhodes University (South Africa)

J. M. Bertran, Reader, Hamburg Universität (Germany)

Dr. Ingrid van Biezen, Reseracher

Dr. G. Blakeley, Head of Department, University of Birmingham (England)

University of Huddersfield (England)

Dr. D. Blondel, Head of Department, London University, Guildhall (England)

Dr. I. Boada-Montagut, Lecturer, University of Ulster, Derry (Eire)

Christian Bollinger, Lecturer, Universität Bern (Switzerland)

Gregory A. Borchard, Instructor, Florida University, Gainsville (USA)

Dr. Stephen Boyd, Lecturer, University College, Cork (Eire)

Dr. Fran Brearton, Lecturer University, Belfast (Eire)

Dr. Malcolm Brown, Lecturer, Queen's University of Exeter (England)

Finlay Bryden, Engineer, University of Glasgow (Scotland)

Magee Burns, Trustee, Women Working Worldwide (England)

Jorge Rodolfo Busch, Enginyer, Universidad de Buenos Aires (Argentina)

Ute Büscher, Lecturer, University of Atlanta (USA)

Dr. Jackie Cannon, Senior Lecturer, Oxford Brookes University (England)

Gonzalo Cano Hernández, librarian, Universidad de Canarias (Spanish State)

Mirella Cantrill, Lecturer, Nottingham Trent University (England)

Dr. A. L. Cartwright, Researcher, University of Liverpool (England)

F. L. Carvalho, Researcher, University of Queensland (Australia)

Giacomo Casarino, University Teacher, Università di Genova (Italy)

Antoni Castells i Talens, University Teacher, University of Florida (USA)

Dr. D. Castiglione, Senior Lecturer, University of Exeter (England)

Dr. Miljenko Cemeljic, Lecturer, Potsdam Universität, (Germany)

Dr. Steven Cherry, Lecturer, University of East Anglia, Norwich (England)

Margaret Childers, Director, Spanish Refugee Aid IRC, New York (USA)

Piero Conti, University Teacher, Università di Genova (Italy)

Dr. D. Conversi, Senior Lecturer, University of Lincoln (England)

Dr. Peter Cunich, Lecturer, University of Hong-Kong (Hong-Kong)

Dr. Ann Davis, Director, University of Calgary (Canada)

Johan Deklerck, Lecturer, Katholieke Universiteit Leuven (Belgium)

M. Delgado, Lecturer, Queen Mary's, London University (England)

Maria Deptula, Archivist, American Bible Society, Nida Institute (USA)

Dr. J. Diaz-Cintas, Senior Lecturer, University of Surrey (England)

Dr. Mark Donovan, Senior Lecturer, Cardiff University (Wales)

Andrew Dowling, Historian, London University (England)

Niall Downie, Engineer, Napier University, Edinburgh (Scotland)

Drs. J. van Duijvendijk, University Teacher, Leiden Universiteit (Holland)

Dr. Chris Ealham, Head of Studies, University of Wales, Cardiff (Wales)

Dr. John Edwards, Researcher, Oxford University (England)

Toni Escasany, Educator, Derby University (England)

Patxi Etxeberria Mendia, University Teacher, Presidente de ALDEE (Basque Country)

J. A. Fernàndez, Lecturer, Queen Mary's, London University (England)

Dr. Antony Fluxman, University Teacher, Rhodes University (South Africa)

Dr. C. Fracchia, Course Director, Birkbeck College, London University (England)

Per Franberg, University Teacher, Umea University (Sweden)

Giuliana Franchini, Researcher, Università di Genova (Italy)

Dr. Fort Fu-Te Liao, University Teacher, Sinica Academy (Taiwan)

Alexander Gabriles, Engineer, Houston, Texas (USA)

Mariano García Ruipérez, Archivist, Archivo Municipal, Toledo (Spanish State)

Victoria L. Garcia, Lecturer, Princeton University (USA)

Brian Garman, Lecturer, Rhodes University (South Africa)

Dr. Harry Garuba, Lecturer, Cape Town University (South Africa)

B. Gaya i Roqueta, Lecturer, Queen Mary's London University (England)

Dr. Lawrence M. Geary, Lecturer, University College, Cork (Eire)

Dr. Sharif Gemie, Senior Lecturer, Glamorgan University (Wales)

Jim George, Senior Lecturer, The Australian National University (Australia)

Robert Germay, Director, Théâtre Universitaire, Université de Liège (Belgium)

Dr. J. W. Gilmour, Senior Lecturer, University of Bristol (England)

Dr. Paul Goalen, Lecturer, Cambridge University (England)

Dr. Peter Gold, Head of Department, University of W. England, Bristol (England)

Olga Gómez, Teaching Fellow, Lancaster University (England)

Auke van der Goot, Historian, Ministry of the Interior (Holland)

Aitor Goti Elondi, University Teacher, Euskal Herriko Unibertsitatea (Basque Country)

Dr. Colin Graham, Lecturer, Queen's University, Belfast (Eire)

Dr. A. Gruenfelder, Diplomat, Austrian Embassy, Zagreb (Croatia)

Celio Gutiérrez Ascano, Psychopedagogue, Canarias (Spanish State)

Dr. C. Gutiérrez, Archive Director, Universidad Católica del Perú (Peru)

Dr. Harvey J. Hames, Lecturer, University of the Negev Beersheba (Israel)

Dr. Ameur-Zaïmèche Haoua, University Teacher, Université Paris I (France)

Dr. D. Hardiman, Research Fellow, University of Warwick (England)

Kelley Hargrave, Linguist, Austin, Texas (USA)

Dr. R. Harrison, Senior Lecturer, Manchester University (England)

Dr. Harshyl Hartman, Director, The Sholem Community, Los Angeles (USA)

Dr. Moyra Haslett, University Teacher, Queen's University, Belfast (Eire)

Dr. Coen Helderman, Historian, Erasmus Universiteit, Rotterdam (Holland)

Robert Hooworth-Smith, Lecturer, University of Lincoln (USA)

Dr. Eamonn Hughes, Lecturer, Queen's University, Belfast (Eire)

Dr. Steven Hurst, Lecturer, Manchester Metropolitan University (England)

Dr. Atsuko Ichijo, R.P. Officer, London School of Economics (England)

Koldo Izagirre, Writer, Armiarma Web (Basque Country)

P. Jardí Soler, Reader, Universität Wien (Àustria)

Dr. D. Javakhishvili, Lecturer, Tbilisi State University (Georgia)

Dr. Louise Johnson, University Teacher, University of Sheffield (England)

Dr. Bill Jones, Lecturer, Cardiff University (Wales)

Clarence Kailin, War Veteran, The Lincoln Brigades, Wisconsin (USA)

Dr. S. Katzenellenbogen, Senior Lecturer, University of Manchester (England)

Dr. B. Kelleher, Director, University of Ulster, Newtonabbey (Eire)

Dr. Brian Kelly, Lecturer, Queen's University, Belfast (Eire)

Dr. William Kenefick, Lecturer, University of Dundee (Scotland)

Dr. Stewart King, Lecturer, Monash University (Australia)

Katerina Kitsi-Mitakou, University Teacher, Aristotle University of Thessaloniki (Greece)

Dr. Tess Knighton, Researcher, Cambridge University (England)

Dr. Vanessa Knights, Lecturer, University of Newcastle (England)

Rosaan Kruger, Lecturer, Rhodes University (South Africa)

Dr. Giuliana Laschi, University Teacher, Università degli Studi di Bologna (Italy)

Dr. P. Lassman, Senior Lecturer, University of Birmingham (England)

John Lawlor, Cinematographer, Narbona (France)

Dr. Stefano Levati, Researcher, Università degli Studi de Milano (Italy)

Barry Lipton, Computer Scientist, Toronto University (Canada)

Peter Lotto, ex Lincoln Brigadier, Lincoln Brigades Association (USA)

David Lynn, Conservationist, Grimes Eyak Council, Alaska (USA)

Eoghann MacColl, Artist, Dunlop, Ayrshire (Scotland)

N. MacQueen, Head of Department, University of Dundee (Scotland)

Dr. J. Mallea-Olaetxe, Historian, University of Nevada (USA)

Tandori Maria, Archivist, SZTE, Torteneti Szakkonyvtar (Hungary)

Suzana Marjanic, Anthropologist

Ed Martin, Adjunct Instructor, IEFR Zagreb (Croatia)

Clayton College & State University (USA)

Dr. P. Masque, Fulbright Scientist, Stony Brook University, (USA)

Dr. J. Mayo, Head of Department, University of the West Indies (Barbados)

K. McColl, Political Researcher, Ayrshire (Scotland)

Dr. Ann McFall, Lecturer, Heriot-Watt University, Edinburgh (Scotland)

Dr. Michael McKinley, University Teacher, Australian National University (Australia)

Poly Miliori, Journalist and Writer, Athens (Greece)

Martina Milla Bernad, Lecturer, Emory University (USA)

Dr. Peter Monteath, Lecturer, University of South Australia, Flinders (Australia)

Dr. Kevin Moore, Lecturer, Lincoln University (New Zealand)

Dr. Cornelia Navari, University Teacher, Birmingham University (England)

Mary Ann Newman, Translator, New York (USA)

Dr. Scott Newton, Senior Lecturer, Cardiff University (Wales)

Dr. Karoline Noack, Lecturer, Freie Universität, Berlin (Germany)

Dr. P. O'Riagáin, ECMI adviser, Institiúid Teangeolaíochta Éireann (Eire)

Dr. Patricia O'Bryne, Lecturer, Dublin City University (Eire)

M. O'Callaghan, President, Global Vision Corporation, Wicklow (Eire)

Dr. Clare O'Halloran, Lecturer, University of Cork (Eire)

Dr. Tim P. O'Neill, Lecturer, University College, Dublin (Eire)

M. Ortega Hegg, Director, Universidad de Centroamérica, UCA (Nicaragua)

Fraser Otanelli, Journalist, University of South Florida (USA)

Lennart Palmqvist, Archaeologist, Stockholm University (Sweden)

Dr. Tuija Parvikko, Reader, University of Tampere (Finland)

Dr. Maren Petersen, Lecturer, Hamburg Universität (Germany)

Daniel Pfeiffer, Computer Scientist, Universitat Pau Sabatièr, Tolosa (France)

Colleen A. Phelan, UNO Archivist, United Nations Organization, Manhattan (USA)

Robert Phillipson, Lecturer, Copenhagen Business School (Denmark)

Silvana Piga, Archivist, Universidad de San Andrés (Argentina)

Olga Prolifi, Official Delegate, EEC (Belgium)

Marta Rauret, Reader, University of Jerusalem (Israel)

Jan ReinhartLibrary Manager, Rutgers University (USA)

Gala Rebés, Co-ordinator, Red Internacional de Derechos Humanos (Spanish State)

Remedios Rey de las Peñas, Archivist, Archives Department, Huelva (Spanish State)

Dr. A. Ritlyova, Head of Department, Presovska University (Slovenia)

Dr. R. Rix, Head of Department, Leeds University (England)

Daniel Roberts, Lecturer, Queen's University, Belfast (Eire)

C. Roch-Cunill, Researcher, Vancouver University (Canada)

Ignacio Rodríguez Temiño Archaeologist, Àrea de Arqueología / Junta de Andalucía (Spanish State)

Dr. S. Romans-Roca, Lecturer, University of W. England, Bristol (England)

Johan Jacobus Roodt, Lecturer, Rhodes University (South Africa)

Monty J. Roodt, Lecturer, Rhodes University (South Africa)

Jordi Ros, Researcher, University of California, Irvine (USA)

M. C. Rosenzweig, Chief Archivist, Reference Center for Marxist Studies, NY (USA)

Dr. J. P. Rubies, Lecturer, London School of Economics (England)

Philip Runkel, Master Archivist, Marquette University (USA)

Dr. Magnus Ryner, Lecturer, Brunel University (England)

E. de Saint-Martin, Lecturer, Cape Town University (South Africa)

Dr. James Sandham, Lecturer, Oxford University (England)

M. Victoria San Sebastián Muro, Archivist, Archive Department (Basque Country)

Hamamoto Satoko, Researcher, Kyoto University (Japan)

Fabienne Silva, Librarian, Université de Genève (Switzerland)

Mary Simons, Visiting Fellow, Queen's University, Ontario (Canada)

Dr. Carsten Sinner Lecturer, Potsdam University (Germany)

Dr. Tove Skutnabb-Kangas, University Teacher, Roskilde University (Denmark)

Dr. Nathaniel Smith, University Teacher, Franklin and Marshall College, Lancaster (USA)

Warren Snowball, Senior Lecturer, Rhodes University (South Africa)

Dr. Suzanne Spencer, Lecturer, University of Lincoln, Nebraska (USA)

Dr. Eugen Stancu, Lecturer, Central European University, Budapest (Hungary)

R. Summy, Research Consultant, University of Queensland (Australia)

Chris Szejnmann, Reader, University of Leicester (England)

E. H. Taddei, Coordinator, CLACSO, Buenos Aires (Argentina)

Dr. Laitia Tamata, Lecturer, University of the South Pacific (Fiji)

Dr. D. Tambakis, Lecturer, Cambridge University (England)

Guy Thompson, Reader, University of Warwick (England)

Nilda Tincopa Montoya, Human Rights Official, Defensa Campesina, EDAC (Peru)

T. Tinsley, Head of Communications, (CILT) Bedfordbury (England)

Dr. Sergio Torres, University Teacher, Universidad Javeriana, Bogotà (Columbia)

Margaret A. Townsend, Congress Official, Professional Congress Circuit (Spanish State)

Dr. John Turner, Lecturer, Lincoln University (New Zealand)

Dr. L. Twomey, Head of Department, University of Northumbria, Newcastle (England)

Dra. Elsa M. Uribe, Coordinator, Universidad Javeriana, Bogotà (Columbia)

Dr. Rogelio Vallejo, Senior Tutor, University of Bristol (England)

Dr. Viviana Valz, Head Psychologist, Comisión de la Verdad (Peru)

F. S. J. Weitenberg, University Teacher, Centrum Rijksuniversiteit, Groningen (Holland)

Dr. Caragh Wells, Lecturer, University of Bristol (England)

Dr. Julia Wells, Senior Lecturer, Rhodes University (South Africa)

Dr. Anne M. White, Lecturer, Bradford University (England)

Dr. Karin Willemse, Lecturer, Erasmus University, Rotterdam (Holland)

Kate Williams, Lecturer, University of Wales, Aberystwyth (Wales)

Glyn Williams, Reader, University of Wales, Cardiff (Wales)

Sylvia Wirth, Librarian, Bibliothèque de l'Antiquité, Genève (Switzerland)

CATALAN INSTITUTIONS GIVING THEIR SUPPORT TO THE DIGNITY COMMISSION BY WAY OF MOTIONS, GRANTS, CO-OPERATION OR COMMUNICATIONS

Parlament de Catalunya
Diputació de Barcelona
Diputació de Lleida
Diputació de Girona
Associació Catalana Municipis i Comarques
Federació de Municipis de Catalunya
Institut d'Estudis Ilerdencs
Consell Comarcal del Montsià
Consell Comarcal del Vallès Oriental
City councils of the following cities and towns: Albinyana, Alcanar, Alella, Alpens, Altafulla, Amer, Amposta, Arbúcies, Arenys de Munt, Argentona, Artesa de Segre, Badalona, Balsareny, Banyoles, Barberà de la Conca, Barcelona, Begur, Bellcaire d'Empordà, Bellver de Cerdanya, Bigues i Riells, Bràfim, Caldes de Montbui, Calella de la Costa, Cambrils, Campdevànol, Campllong, Camprodon, Cardedeu, Castellcir, Castellet i la Gornal, Castellnou de Seana, Castellterçol, Castellví de Rosanes, Cervera, Conesa, Creixell, Darnius, El Bruc, El Lloar, El Lluçà, El Pla de Santa Maria, El Poal, El Pont de Vilomara, El Prat de Llobregat, El Vendrell, Falset, Figaró-Montmany, Figueres, Flix, Freginals, Garcia, Gavà, Granollers, Igualada, Isona i Conca Dellà, Jafre, La Bisbal de Falset, La Bisbal del Penedès, La Fatarella, La Garriga, La Roca del Vallès, La Selva de Mar, La Seu d'Urgell, Les Borges Blanques, Les Masies de Roda, Les Masies de Voltregà, Linyola, Llagostera, Llardecans, Lleida, Llers, Maçanet de la Selva, Manresa, Martorelles, Masquefa, Molins de Rei, Mollerussa, Mollet, Montblanc, Montmaneu, Montornès del Vallès, Móra d'Ebre, Nulles, Olèrdola, Olesa, Palafrugell, Palau d'Anglesola, Palau-solità i Plegamans, Papiol, Parlavà, Peralada, Piera, Prats de Lluçanès, Premià de Dalt, Premià de Mar, Puigcerdà, Puigverd de Lleida, Rabós d'Empordà, Rajadell, Regencós, Reus, Riudarenes, Riudecols, Riudellots de la Selva, Riudoms, Riumors, Rocafort de Queralt, Roquetes, Roses, Rubí, Sabadell, Sallent, Salomó, Salt, Sant Bartomeu del Grau, Sant Boi de Llobregat, Sant Carles de la Ràpita, Sant Celoni, Sant Cugat, Sant Esteve de Palautordera, Sant Feliu de Guíxols, Sant Feliu de Llobregat, Sant Fruitós del Bages, Sant Gregori, Sant Hilari Sacalm, Sant Hipòlit de Voltregà, Sant Iscle de Vallalta, Sant Pere de Ribes, Sant Pere de Riudebitlles, Sant, uirze del Vallès, Sant Sadurní d'Anoia, Sant Sadurní d'Osomort, Santa Bàrbara, Santa

Coloma de Farners, Santa Coloma de Queralt, Santa Fe del Penedès, Santa Margarida i els Monjos, Santa Maria de Palautordera, Santa Pau, Santa Perpètua de la Mogoda, Santa Perpètua del Gaià, Sentmenat, Sitges, Siurana d'Empordà, Solivella, Sort, Sudanell, Tagamanent, Tarragona, Terrassa, Torà, Tordera, Torelló, Torrebesses, Torredembarra, Torrelles de Llobregat, Torroella de Montgrí, Tortellà, Tortosa, Tremp, Valls, Vic, Viladrau, Vilajuïga, Vila-Sacra, Vilassar de Dalt, Vilassar de Mar, Vimbodí, Vinebre.

THE «SALAMANCA PAPERS», LITMUS PAPERS FOR THE STATE OF SPAIN. A PAPER READ AT SOUTHAMPTON AND SHEFFIELD UNIVERSITIES BY PROFESSOR HENRY ETTINGHAUSEN (NOVEMBER 2002)*

Remember Victor Kayam, the guy who liked the electric razor so much that he decided to buy the company? Well, having professed Hispanism in Southampton for nearly all my working life, when I retired last year we moved to the Empordà. Since when I have been impressed to see how, not just in Catalonia, but in many parts of Spain, the nearly forty years of Francoist repression have finally — shamefully belatedly — become a public issue.

While Franco and José Antonio are still revered by diehard Fascists (and not only Spanish ones) at their tombs in the grotesque Valle de los Caídos, built by forced labour after the Civil War, there has recently been a spate of initiatives to revive Spain's collective historical memory and to counter the amnesia imposed by Francoism. These have included numerous books and newspaper articles on the Francoist prison regime and forced labour; much-publicised (but largely unsuccessful) attempts on the part of 80- and 90-year-old survivors to obtain recognition — even documentation — of their wartime and post-war imprisonment, let alone compensation; documentaries on the forcible and permanent separation of children from their mothers who were prisoners in Franco's jails; the opening by King Juan Carlos of an exhibition in Madrid on the exile of supporters of the Republic; the erection of monuments to the victims of the repression, including (in December) one to the thousands of men and women executed in Seville; and efforts to locate and dig up the mass graves of executed prisoners, notably in León and Galicia. It is not clear to me why all this is happening just now, but it could well be, in part at least, because of the extraordinarily effective campaign that began in spring 2002 for the return of the «Salamanca Papers» that were seized in Catalonia at the end of the Civil War.

The «Papers de Salamanca», officially known as the «Archivo General de la Guerra Civil», are housed in the Monastery of St. Ambrose, in Salamanca — ironically, and to be precise, at c/ Gibraltar, 2 — and represent one of the ugliest fruits of Franco's «crusade» to purge Spain of all organisations and individuals who resisted the military uprising of July 1936 or who might have challenged his dictatorship after the Republic's defeat.

---

* Professor Henry Ettinghausen (Professor Emeritus of Southampton University) is spokesman for the international signatories of the 2002 Manifesto.

Within months of the beginning of the military rebellion, Franco had ordered the destruction of all pub publications found by his Nationalist troops that could be deemed to be contrary to the principles of the 'Movimiento', especially socialist, communist, anarchist, separatist and Masonic literature. As his forces advanced through Spain, publishers' and newspaper offices, bookshops and libraries were combed for works considered to be subversive. Apart from a few copies of such publications that were retained for reference, the rest were to be pulped. In summer 1937 the blandly named 'Oficina de Recuperación de Documentos' was set up with the aim of seizing and processing documentation solely in order to persecute the new regime's enemies. The result is the Salamanca archive, which includes tons of documents seized, not only in Catalonia, but in all those parts of Spain that had resisted the Nationalists' advance, including Bilbao, Santander, Aragon, Madrid, Valencia and Extremadura.

When Barcelona fell on 26 January 1939, the city was immediately divided into ten sectors for the seizure of publications and archives. This work was carried out by a special detachment of about a hundred men, supported by the police and members of the Falange. Their chief targets in Barcelona were the archives of the Generalitat, the Basque government in exile and the Catalan Parliament, as well as the offices of municipalities, political parties, trades unions, schools, cultural associations (including choirs and vegetarian and sporting societies) and the private libraries and papers of prominent intellectuals and political figures. Altogether, some 1,400 separate searches were conducted in Barcelona alone, and 3,500 sacks of seized material were sent by rail to Salamanca, where Franco had set up his HQ in the Bishop's Palace. There they were to form part of the huge police archive that was later christened the Archivo General de la Guerra Civil. The only research produced at this archive was some three million file cards, generated from the materials that had been seized, which were used well into the 50s for «la limpieza de gente perniciosa» — i.e. the imprisonment or execution of the Franco State's enemies.

Demands for the return of those «Papers de Salamanca» that had been stolen at gunpoint in Catalonia were first voiced in 1978 and have been made repeatedly over the years. They appeared to be on the point of achieving their aim in 1995 when the PSOE government resolved to take the appropriate decision, but the Socialist mayor of Salamanca brought out the biggest public demonstration that city had ever seen, a meeting that was addressed by the novelist Gonzalo Torrente Ballester, who assured his listeners that the «Salamanca Papers» were theirs by right of conquest. The decision to return the Catalan materials had not been acted on by the time the Partido Popular won the 1996 elections, but the PP government was eventually persuaded to set up a committee (which, incidentally, did not include a single archivist) to pronounce upon the matter. Last July the committee announced that it had ruled against the return of a single item on the grounds that the unity of the Salamanca archive must be preserved. As the Minister of Education and Culture put it: «La historia de España no se puede fragmentar.» Not content with having won the Civil War, *El Adelanto de Salamanca* boasted the headline: «Salamanca gana la "guerra" del Archivo.»

In anticipation of the committee's decision, the 'Comissió de la Dignitat' was constituted in spring 2002 to raise awareness of the issue both in Catalonia and abroad, achieving the support of over 700 non-Catalan academics and numerous international notables, such as Noam Chomsky, Francesco Cossiga, Rigoberta Menchú, Georges Moustaki, Mario Soares and Mikis Theodorakis. In the wake of the decision to return none of the materials, the «Comissió de la Dignitat» flew 150 prominent Catalan politicians (from all parties except the PP), trades union leaders, mayors, MPs, Senators and journalists to Salamanca on 14 October — the day before an exhibition on wartime propaganda was due to be opened at the Archivo General de la Guerra Civil as part of the «Salamanca, Cultural Capital of Europe, 2002» programme. The aim of the visit was to put the case for the return of the Catalan materials to the Salamanca city and county authorities, but the latter boycotted the event en masse, though it later transpired that the invitation had deliberately been kept secret from many of the city's councillors. As a result, there was not even a dialogue of the deaf, though the local press did turn up and heard a dozen moving speeches — among them those by Carles Fonseré, the 84-year-old sole survivor from among the creators of the famous Republican propaganda posters, who had had the entire contents of his studio seized, and Rosa Maria Carrasco, a CiU member of the Catalan Parliament, whose father's last letters, written moments before his execution in Burgos jail, are believed to be amongst the «Salamanca Papers». Before leaving Salamanca, the Catalan delegation placed a wreath at the door of the Archivo in memory of those who had suffered persecution on the basis of its contents, sang «Els Segadors» and heard Casals' «Cant dels Ocells» played by a young violinist. As they were about to leave, an old man on a balcony behind them shouted out: «¡Aquí están, y aquí se quedarán!» — the only direct response to the visit that they obtained that day. The following day the Salamanca press either virtually ignored the event or else treated it with contempt. One of the local papers, *Tribuna,* featured an editorial headed "El insulto nacionalista catalán" which railed and ranted against the visiting Catalans for supposedly wanting to disinter the ghost of the Civil War, scorning Salamanca's hospitality and bringing along posters in Catalan.

However, at least three Salmantinos had the decency and the guts to stand up and be counted: the Socialist Councillor Teresa Carvajal, who protested at not having been informed by the Salamanca authorities of the invitation to attend the meeting; Aníbal Lozano, a regular contributor to *Tribuna*, who had his daily column reduced to a weekly for having published an article shortly before the visit supporting the Catalan campaign; and José Frías, Director of the Departamento de Biblioteconomía y Documentación at the University of Salamanca, who likewise expressed the view that the spoils of war should be returned to their rightful owners.

To most Catalans the Spanish government's refusal to hand the papers back feels like the deliberate perpetuation of a State act of armed robbery. It is a feeling that is strengthened by the PP's distaste for Catalan nationalism, which it often brackets with Basque nationalism, and so, by implication, with ETA terrorism. Nor — to give one instance of the survival of attitudes supposedly superseded by the transition to democracy — is the feeling lessened by the fact that the Bishop's Palace in Salamanca still bears a stone plaque engraved with the inscription: «Aquí vivió y dirigió nuestra Cruzada Nacional el Caudillo Franco. La Diputación Provincial de Salamanca.» An even more shocking instance, revealed as a result of the Catalans' campaign to get their property back, is the fact that the private foundation that receives the greatest (but unpublicised) subvention from the Spanish State is the Fundación Nacional Francisco Franco — an organisation whose website proclaims that its aims and objectives include defending «la legitimidad del Alzamiento Nacional», commemorating Franco's death and «difundir el conocimiento de Francisco Franco en sus dimensiones humana, política y militar.»

Having followed these events over the past few months and attended several meetings organised by the Comissió de la Dignitat in my capacity as one of its many foreign supporters, I have had occasion to mull over the arguments on both sides. One of them — the «archivistic» argument — comes down to the Spanish government's decision to favour the unity of the sinister Salamanca archive over that of the hundreds of archives whose unity was violated in order o create it. Another — which we could call the legal argument — involves the Spanish government's apparent desire to give greater weight to the principle of «derecho de conquista» than to the right of those robbed to have their stolen property returned. A third — let's call it the 'comparative' argument — links the case of the «Salamanca Papers» to that of the Elgin Marbles and ignores the fact that UNESCO has repeatedly pronounced in favour of returning documents seized in time of war and the fact that (however belatedly) some attempt is finally being made to return to their rightful owners, or their descendents, works of art that were looted by the Nazis. Finally, there's the political argument, which could be summarised as «Let sleeping dogs lie» vs. «Why let lying dogs sleep?» Ultimately, this seems to me to boil down to a moral question. Refusing to return the Catalan papers — doing nothing — is not a neutral decision. It is a decision to do *something*: to seek to maintain collective amnesia and to rule out remedying one of the very few disasters of the Civil War that can still be remedied.

A few weeks ago Josep Piqué, the PP's candidate for President de la Generalitat, declared that «¡La España de hoy es la que los catalanes queríamos! ¡La España de hoy se ha hecho catalana!» Meanwhile, the Spanish government goes on indulging in what ought to be an embarrassingly gross nationalistic ceremony that it introduced just a few months ago: the raising of a 300-square-metre Spanish flag on a massive flagpole in the Plaza de Colón in the centre of Madrid on the first Wednesday of every month. But the Comissió de la Dignitat's dignified and impressive campaign goes on too.

This text is a revised version of a paper given at the Universities of Southampton and Sheffield in November 2002. The author is grateful for background information supplied by Josep Cruanyes.

THE ARTICLE «WRITTEN IN BLOOD», WRITTEN BY TIM ABRAHAMS AND ILLUSTRATED BY COLIN MEARNS, WHICH APPEARED IN *THE HERALD*, GLASGOW, ON SATURDAY 13 APRIL 2002

Written in blood

Once General Franco used them to violently repress his Republican foes.

Now the Catalan victims of the Salamanca Papers want them back

Words TIM ABRAHAMS

Photographs COLIN MEARNS

Amid the metallic blossom of cranes that have sprung up along Barcelona's Mediterranean shore stands a memorial. Today it is belittled by the jungle of higher structures that are building Barcelona's bold, bright future, but it commemorates a period of the city's recent past. Between 1939 to 1952, 1,704 people were shot here by General Franco.

Cassandra Mestre remembers the day when her brother was shot on this spot on February 17, 1949. A small, modest 78-year-old, she reveals an impenetrable resilience as she peels back the years. When Franco began his aerial bombardment of the city, her father was in hiding. He had been involved in the movement to create co-operative farms and factories. His card, as they say, was marked. At 14, Cassandra fled to France with her mother in pursuit of their brother who had volunteered for the army at 15. They didn't find him and their father was captured as he came to meet them in France. He was sentenced to death for his left-wing loyalties.

«My father was held with all the other condemned men in an underground dungeon,» she says. «The guards would wake them up and read out a list of names as if they were about to be shot. Some of them would be executed. Some of them wouldn¹t. They played this game with him for six months.» Her father's sentence was eventually commuted when a former Francist colleague intervened. Cassandra's brother wasn't so lucky. Like many Catalans, he fought with the French Resistance against the collaborationist government throughout the war, but when he continued his subterfuge against the Spanish state there was no support from the Allies.

Numen Mestre was caught in 1949. He was 26, with a decade of combat experience already behind him. «My father went to see the man who had saved his life and asked him, «Can you help my son as you helped me?» and he was told, «No. I did it for you, but I won't do it for him. He came into the country to kill Francists like me.» Which I suppose is true. So they shot my brother.»

It isn't just the memorial at Diagonal Mar which will immortalise the sacrifice her brother and others made to try and defeat Fascism. Some 500 miles away across the barren plain of northern Spain is a small room, filled with filing cabinets and decorated solely with a reproduction of the most famous image of the Spanish Civil War, Picasso's Guernica. Inside the cabinets are three million brown index cards; one of which has the name Numen Mestre on it. Each name is followed by a simple description. «Antonio San Jose. A sergeant in the air force,» reads one, randomly selected. «On July 19 he enrolled in the 5th Regiment, later becoming part of the brigade led by the general known as El Campesino, where he distinguished himself in morale and combat. In June 1937, he became a pilot at 17 years of age and was known as the Youngest Pilot of the Glorious.» There is no indication as to what eventually happened to Antonio. He may have been shot or tortured. He may be retired somewhere, having lived a relatively normal life, except for those days in his youth when he fought in a war which has fascinated the the world ever since.

These are the Salamanca Blood Papers. Together with the documents used as a source of information, they are the physical remains of the repression meted out to his opponents by General Franco. Collectively they are officially called the Archive of the Civil War, created when Franco organised an unprecedented system of information-gathering about his political opponents. His wily minister of the interior, Serrano Súñer, sent his police force, the Guardia Civil, into public buildings, the offices of trade unions and private homes to seize papers whenever the Fascist army took a town. In Salamanca, they then drew up a blacklist of «anti-Spanish elements», before returning to the centres of opposition and executing, imprisoning or conscripting individuals into the army or forced work battalions.

For more than 60 years these cards have sat in this beautiful eighteenth-century building. «Madrid was Republican,» explains archive director Miguel Jaramillo, «and Salamanca represented a perfect image of Spanish traditions. Franco wanted to regain the imperial past and all the images of it were here; the rule of the Catholic kings, the tradition of the university and the spirituality of the great thinkers who have sat there.»

Salamanca is still a beautiful city. As charming a university town as Cambridge with more impressive buildings and fewer students. In 1254, Pope Alexander IV called the University of Salamanca «one of the four leading lights of the world», but the attack on free thought during the Inquisition saw its prestige decline and the city never fully recovered its standing. This year, though, it is the European City of Culture and the Salamantines see the archive as part of their cultural wealth.

To the Catalans, however, the papers represent war booty stolen by the Spanish state. A campaign led by Catalan nationalists is calling for the documents relating to Catalan history to be returned. They claim them not just by right of practical necessity and symbolism, but because the government of Madrid first promised their return in 1979, even before they granted Catalonia autonomy.

Director of the Catalonian National Archive, Josep Maria Sans i Travé, supports their goal. «That this documentation remains sequestered in Salamanca without having been returned to its legitimate owners means the Civil War is not yet over,» he says. Paul Preston, a British historical expert on the Spanish Civil War, concurs. «The failure of the Salamanca archive to return this documentation to its rightful owners is scandalous. The argument that it now constitutes a valuable archive seems to me a spurious one».

Cassandra Mestre gives a derisive snort when asked what she thinks should happen to the papers. «They should be here in Catalonia, of course.» Unlike historians, however, she wants them returned because they represent the system that killed her brother and subjected her father to torment. Perhaps, too, it's caused by a resentment towards the Spain that invaded Barcelona, a Spain that she believes still lives on.

In one of the filing cabinets lies a card with the name Josep Sanjoan Güell on it. He has never seen it. Sitting in the home of his historian friend Antoni Gavaldà, he remembers the day when that same friend told him that his trade union activity had been immortalised in the archive. «The most important trade union in our area was the Confederacion Nacional del Trabajo, but they were in the hands of the anarchists. Some of my fellow iron workers didn't agree with their politics so we opened a branch of Unió General de Treballadors. It was a union formed in Barcelona in 1888, but I was the founder of the branch in Valls in 1937,» he says with no small amount of pride.

Sitting in Gavaldà's home, in the tranquil town of Valls, he remembers the time he travelled the 500 miles west to see the archive. «Fifteen years ago when Toni first told me that he had seen my papers when he was writing his thesis I was curious. I said to my wife that we should go to Salamanca to see my papers and see my name. I went to the main entrance. At first I admired this strange building, then I thought of those sad days. But I was satisfied. I didn¹t feel the need to go in.» This is, perhaps, just as well because only historians and journalists are allowed into the archive.

Smiling frequently, Güell doesn't boil with the same anger as those Catalans who so vociferously demand the return of the papers, yet were too young to have fought in the war. «I don't complain that the Spanish put me in a concentration camp or made me work in the forced labour battalions. That was the price of our defeat. Now, I am proud that my name appears in the archive. It is the curriculum vitae of a good socialist,» he says with a glint in his eye.

When Franco's slow progress across Spain took him to the gates of Catalonia, Güell saw fighting as the logical continuation of his union activity. Then, as he was moving from one battlefront to another, his truck was bombed and he was injured. «I was lucky, however, because I was put in a military hospital in Barcelona. From there I could go into exile in France when I recovered. I remember the exact day I went into exile. It was February 5, 1939, my nineteenth birthday.»

Nearly half a million Spaniards crossed the border into France, only to suffer in concentration camps on the beaches of Argelers. Güell preferred to return to Spain. It was then that Franco's police caught up with him. He was arrested and put in the forced work battalion.

«I worked as slave labour. We worked our way across the whole of Spain. From the Basque country in the north, to Cadiz in the south, building roads, bunkers and bridges, with disgusting food and terrible conditions. It took me three years.»

After two years in the Francist army in conditions that were just as bad, Güell returned home to continue his union activity in secrecy. His presence in the archive was only revealed when Gavaldà found his name while writing his university thesis on a famous local anarchist. Gavaldà remembers the shock of his first experience of looking through the documents. «The organisation of the archive is terrible. There are so many documents that are not in order. I asked for a file on the city of Tarragona, but I found papers from Galicia and other parts of Spain in it».

Another historian shows us copies of papers that originated in Mexico in a file supposedly from Barcelona. «About 25 per cent of this documentation is in Catalan,» continues Gavaldà. «We only want what was stolen from us. It costs a lot of money for a local historian like me to go to Salamanca to research information about events that occurred in the very town I live in.»

Güell is glad that he paid the price, however. Franco's regime must have been a long winter for the Republicans who fought him, particularly the Catalans who were forbidden from speaking their own language during his regime. They had waited with hope when the Second World War finished to see if Franco would be removed by the Allies, along with Hitler and Mussolini, only to be disappointed. They were confounded further when Spain was admitted to the United Nations in 1955 and when President Eisenhower visited Madrid in 1959 to grant the next instalment of aid which eventually totalled $2bn. Up until the last year of his life, Franco cowed the opposition by executing around 200,000 people, on top of those who had died in the Civil War, many of them for less than Güell's union activity. «The work that Toni did is very important,» says Güell. «Through his study he can tell many people what he knows about Valls. On a personal level, I am very grateful to Toni for his work. I have learned things about Valls during the Civil War that I never knew, even though I was alive at the time. More importantly, though, people who want to learn about what happened here where we stood and why we fought ? can read Toni's work.»

It is no mistake that Catalans are calling for the papers return. Xavier Farré, a Catalan historian, describes the Spanish Civil War, as the sequel to the War of the Reapers which began in 1640 (where Catalonia lost land which is now part of the French state) and the War of Spanish Succession in 1714 (where the remainder of Catalonia was incorporated more fully into the Spanish state). «When the French monarchy took our papers in the seventeenth century they reallocated them to various archives, some to the new departments created by the French, some to the treasury, some to the national archives. They were assimilated. As a consequence the memories of the Catalans in southern France have successfully been separated from the real past. «The Spanish state did something different, however. They retained the papers taken from us as a separate entity, simply because they didn't realise how important they were. If the Spanish Guardia Civil had done their job properly, we would have no opportunity to regain our memory.»

Surely though, with the advent of microfilm, the physical papers are no longer as vital? Heribert Barrera disagrees. He fought Francist forces during the Civil War and organised Catalan resistance in the post-war years. Now 85, he is seen as the «last link» by Catalan Nationalists. He says that is simply because he was one of the few who survived. He stood as a deputy of the Catalan Parliament when it was restored in 1980, as a member of the Esquerra Republicana, a Catalan nationalist party, and was elected as President. His details, and those of his father who was a minister in the last Republican government before Franco's coup d'etat, sit on a card somewhere in one of those filing cabinets.

«Personally I think their importance is their symbolism,» he says. «If the Salamanca Papers were returned to us, it would be a recognition of our distinct personality as Catalans. It's not the material value of the papers, it's what they mean in the mind of the Catalan people.» The Catalan people, however, have been far more reticent about expressing their mind, compared to the vociferous Salamantines. In Barcelona, not just the capital of Catalonia but one of the major commercial and cultural centres of Europe, the younger generation seems more satisfied with the status quo. Part of the nationalists' urgent need for these documents comes from a concern over this passive response. The constitutional arrangement which was one of the most obvious models for Scottish devolution, fixes Catalonia as a state within a state and for the large part young Catalans seem comfortable with it. Only 40 per cent of the population of Catalonia speak Catalan as their first language, however, and the older generation fears for the future.

Barrera explains: «The only way that we can guarantee that the Catalan nation stays and survives is through independence. If not, we will slowly disappear because in Catalonia we have a big problem which is not the same as Scotland, for example. We are being minoritised in our own country because most of the population is not of Catalan origin. They are from Andalucia and the rest of Spain or they are immigrants from South America and Africa who are increasing the Spanish-speaking portion of our society. If we had independence, we could control language. If you look at France, they have a large number of immigrants from Africa but all of them speak French. All of the immigrants who come to Barcelona speak Spanish not Catalan.»

Of course, it is a generalisation to say that a younger generation is more comfortable with Catalonia's bilingual status and the pros and cons of globalisation while the older wants the Catalan nation guaranteed. There are many young Catalans who know from their parents that the language they now speak freely was once illegal.

Whatever the age, however, it's difficult not to feel sympathy with anyone who expresses that they would like to see the papers returned, given the Spanish state's reluctance to organise the papers better. A special board is currently contemplating whether to expand the archive to make it a more complete record of the era rather than leaving it simply as the remains of a system of repression or to return it.

As an outsider, it is hard to see why the papers should not be returned to Catalonia. The cards, on the other hand, listing the deeds of each enemy of Franco and which were written in Spain, could arguably stay were they are, with an important qualification. If the Salamantines do not want to lose them, they should use them. The fact that a foreign journalist was permitted to wander among these simple testimonies, all the more powerful for having been written by a totalitarian regime, while those whose lives are actually detailed there are not permitted to do so is nonsensical. Perhaps, though, the memories such an exhibition would rekindle are more than Spain, despite its new prosperity, could bear.